Wrestling Wit

A CONVERT'S TALE

Wrestling With the Angel
A CONVERT'S TALE

Jon Elsby

_____cHp_____
CentreHouse Press

British Library Cataloguing in Publication Data
A catalogue record for this book is available from
the British Library

ISBN 978-1-902086-09-5

Printed and bound by Lightning Source
Cover images courtesy Shutterstock

CONTENTS

Introduction

On the 29th June 2001, the Feast Day of St Peter and St Paul, I was received into the Roman Catholic Church. I was then forty-six years old.

I had not been raised as a Catholic. My father was a High Church Anglican, my mother a Baptist. For most of my childhood we attended Nonconformist churches. When I was about thirteen, we stopped attending church altogether. About the age of sixteen, I lost my faith and wavered between agnosticism and atheism for most of the next thirty years.

This essay attempts to explain how and why I lost my faith and how and why I recovered it – or, more accurately, it came back to me, for I am not sure that I can claim the honour of having recovered it. I did not take any positive steps to do so. Moreover, when my faith returned, it returned in a form it had never had before: Roman Catholicism. If anyone had asked me at the age of twenty-five what I thought were the chances of my converting to Catholicism, I should have said that there was no chance at all of my doing any such thing. The idea was absurd.

It is well said that God moves in mysterious ways.

The evolutionary biologist, Richard Dawkins, believes that religion is a kind of mental aberration and has tried to account for its persistence in the human race by developing a theory of cultural replicators called 'memes'. Professor Dawkins's speculations have been vigorously debunked by so many thinkers, not all of them Christians, that it is surely unnecessary to add to their number. Indeed, I do not feel inclined to, for I think he may have got hold of a truth. To be sure, he has got hold of it the wrong way round and examined it from every angle except the right one, but he is on to something, just the same. And the something is this. Even the most reasonable people are very seldom argued, by strictly philosophical reasoning, into, or out of, religious belief. If the philosophical arguments serve any purpose at all, it is to bolster, by rationalizing, a belief, or unbelief, which has already been arrived at on other grounds. And in fact the philosophical arguments for or against the existence of God could not very well do anything else because they all beg the question – that is, they assume in their premisses the point that they purport to prove. If anyone disagrees with me, let him examine the philosophical arguments that claim to demonstrate logically the existence of God. Then let him examine the so-called refutations of those arguments advanced by, say, Hume, Feuerbach, Marx, Freud or Sartre. He will not find a single valid argument among them, not one that proves anything at all, which is why the question continues to be debated so intemperately even today, and why all the disputes prove inconclusive. The disputants invariably start from different positions, not infrequently employ different methods of reasoning, and, not surprisingly, arrive at different conclusions.

Of course, the corollary of this is that theism and atheism are equally without a strict philosophical justification. Or that they are equally capable of being 'justified' philosophically, which comes to the same thing. One is left with the problem of what to believe. Perhaps agnosticism is the only rational option? Well, no, because, as I hope to show later, agnosticism too depends on assuming the truth of propositions whose truth is by no means self-evident. There is no default position from which the errors of others can be observed in safety with a sense of Olympian detachment. Moreover, even if there were such a position, philosophy would take us only so far. It would, at most, enable us to decide on rational but not incontrovertible grounds whether theism, atheism or agnosticism offered the most credible explanation of the observable facts of the world around us. But it would not help us to judge whether, as all the monotheistic religions claim, God has made any special revelation to the human race, or to adjudicate between the rival truth claims of the different religions with respect to the nature and content of such a revelation. For that, we must look to another discipline altogether: we must look to revealed theology.

So where does that leave us? It leaves us at the beginning. At the start of a story – in this case, the history of my religious beliefs – which is also an inquiry: an inquiry into what we ought to believe and why.

My Early Life

My Early Life

I was born in Shoreham-by-Sea, West Sussex on 30th May 1955. I was the youngest of three children. My sister Ann was five years older than I, and my brother Andrew four years older. I also had a half-brother, Paul – my father's son from his first marriage, who was twelve years my senior – but he, sadly, did not live with us. My father was English and a civil engineer who specialized in the construction and management of sea ports. We therefore travelled as a family and lived in various countries, wherever major projects of port construction, development or management were to be found. My mother was from a burgher family in Ceylon (as Sri Lanka was then known). Religiously, my father was a High Church Anglican and so were all his family. He had sung in a church choir as a boy and had therefore presumably been a regular churchgoer. My mother, like her own mother, was a Baptist. Her father was a Roman Catholic who had been excommunicated when he married outside the Catholic Church. Many years later, long after my mother had left home and married, my maternal grandmother was received into the Catholic Church, as were my mother's four sisters, all of whom at that stage still lived in Sri Lanka. Initially, my grandmother's decision was motivated by a desire to enable my grandfather to be readmitted to communion with his church, but, having undergone instruction prior to her reception into the Church, she was received as a convinced and committed Catholic. She confirmed as much in a letter to my mother some time afterwards. My mother, however, saw no reason to change her beliefs or her church and therefore remained a Baptist. Neither she nor my father was ever anti-Catholic. Indeed it was not in their nature to be 'anti' anything other than what was, beyond all doubt, morally repellent. They were as nearly devoid of prejudice as anyone I have ever known, and such prejudices as they did have were mild and harmless, not pernicious.

I recall some of the churches we attended. In Singapore, for instance, where we lived for three years when I was between the ages of six and nine, we went first to a Southern Baptist church, where the American minister was so violently opposed to alcohol that he changed all the references to wine in the Bible to 'fermented grapejuice'. My parents both drank in moderation and neither was prepared to listen meekly to violent denunciations from the pulpit of an innocent pleasure. For the rest of our time in Singapore, we attended a Methodist church, which also had an American minister, though one whose views on alcohol were, if not more moderate, at least more private. The Methodist church had the social advantage of being attended by most of our Chinese friends. In Glasgow, where we lived for a year, we went to a Baptist church. I remember only one occasion when we attended an Anglican service (it was, I think, in Southport) and the experiment was not repeated. It was my mother who, wherever we lived, decided what church we should attend. My father had a preference for High Anglican ritual and referred to Nonconformist practices, a little disparagingly, as 'homespun religion'. He respected Nonconformists and their clergy, but their religious practices were not to his taste. My mother, on the other hand, liked her religion homespun. She thought ritual an unnecessary distraction and hierarchies an imposition. In order to justify her mild but firm disapproval of ecclesiastical hierarchies in principle, however benign individual bishops, archbishops, cardinals or popes might be, she would quote Jesus's saying that, in the kingdom of heaven, the first would be last and the last would be first.

And yet among her most treasured possessions was a rosary my grandmother had given her which had been blessed by the Pope.

Apart from my mother's views on the episcopacy and church ritual, another possible reason for our not attending Anglican churches is that my father's first marriage had ended in divorce. It is quite likely therefore that, in those days, he would have been unable to take communion in his own church. And my mother, as a Baptist, would certainly have been ineligible. An ironic postscript to this is that, many years later, after my father's death, my mother resumed the practice of going to church on Sundays. The church she attended, though only because it was the nearest, was – an Anglican church! But, by that time, Anglican doctrine, especially in low churches, had become so diluted that, even though she was a Baptist and wished to remain one (a fact of which she made no secret), she was accepted as a member of the church and allowed to take communion. There is something wryly amusing – and also for me oddly comforting – in the fact that my devout Protestant mother ended her life as a member of a church that has never quite relinquished its claim to be part of the Catholic Church.

When I was fourteen years old, we returned to England after

two and a half years in the United States. My parents sent me to a private Catholic school for boys in Kent,[1] not because they especially wanted to, but because it was difficult to find me a place anywhere else within reach of where we lived. The school had two priests on the staff. Catholic prayers were said at morning assembly and the Catholic boys were expected to attend Mass on holy days of obligation and were questioned closely by the priests if they failed to do so. It was my first contact with Catholicism and everything about it was alien to me. I did not like having to address the priests as 'Father'. It seemed wrong. After all, they weren't my father. I had a father and didn't see why the title hitherto reserved to him should now be bestowed on someone else. I didn't like the disciplined approach to religious observance or the authority wielded by the priests. Religion and religious practice, I thought, should be freely chosen, not authoritatively enforced. At some point, I found a battered copy of the shorter catechism in the school library, read it, and was appalled. The unbaptized who died in infancy were consigned to a place called limbo. Why? Surely infants were innocent? Where was the biblical authority for that teaching? Or for the doctrine of purgatory? There was (to me) an utterly incomprehensible doctrine called transubstantiation. How could anyone believe that? And there were other doctrines I had never so much as heard of – the Immaculate Conception, the Assumption, the Sacrament of Confession. Did Catholics really believe them all? None of these doctrines had formed any part of my religious upbringing. They all seemed to me nothing but the arbitrary inventions of…well, of what exactly? Religious maniacs? Mediæval theologians? Or a powerful, monarchic institution acting to protect and further its interests and to consolidate its power? I adopted quite unreflectively the Protestant conviction that the Catholic Church stood in grave need of reform before reunion would be possible and, after reading the shorter catechism, I doubted that the Church was capable of undertaking the necessary work. It was institutionally irreformable. Its power structures, especially the power vested in the Pope, who was presumed (erroneously, of course) to be infallible, would frustrate any attempt at reform.

Curiously, it never occurred to me to ask how Catholics themselves, many of whom were clearly highly intelligent, might justify their beliefs, if called upon to do so. I simply assumed that their beliefs were without any possible justification because *I* couldn't think of one. It also never occurred to me to ask what authority I had for my own beliefs. They simply appeared to me to be the beliefs of common sense. Someone must have made the world, otherwise why did anything exist rather than nothing? Whoever did must have been a Being of infinite, or at least enormous, power. And we call that Being God. The record of Jesus's life, teaching, death and Resurrection in the Gospels was good evidence for the basic beliefs held in common by all Christians. Anything beyond those common beliefs was otiose and an obstacle to Christian unity. All the beliefs that Catholics held and Protestants rejected fell into this category. Such, in summary, were my religious views at the age of fifteen.

I thought I knew the Gospels fairly well but in fact I didn't. I knew bits of them – mostly very familiar bits like the Sermon on the Mount and some of the better-known parables: the Prodigal Son, the Good Samaritan, and Dives and Lazarus. I knew the stories of the woman taken in adultery, of the feeding of the 5,000, and of Jesus walking on the water; and, like all Christians who have at some time in their lives attended church, I knew the Nativity and Passion narratives. But there was a great deal that I didn't know. I knew nothing of the Eucharistic discourse in Chapter Six of St John's Gospel, for instance. I was unaware of the differences between the Synoptic Gospels and the Fourth Gospel. I knew nothing about the relations between the Old Testament and the New. I knew nothing about the Book of the Apocalypse. I knew nothing of the promises of Christ to the Church. I knew practically nothing of the Pauline epistles, which I found hard going. I thought them repetitive and boring. In fact, I had a prejudice against St Paul not uncommon among Protestants. I regarded him as a fanatic and thought that anything in the epistles was open to question unless corroborated by the Gospels. That St Paul was the first great Christian theologian and also the earliest source for the truths of Christianity – earlier than any of the evangelists – I did not know, and would have been astonished to hear, if anyone had thought to tell me. My ignorance of most of the Bible and all of Christian theology and philosophy did not in any way inhibit the confidence with which I held my beliefs, or my readiness to give others the benefit of my views on the slightest provocation.[2]

And then, when I was about sixteen, everything changed.

I had always been a voracious reader, devouring indiscriminately everything that came within my reach from classics to crime novels. Until I was fourteen, my reading was undertaken under my mother's supervision. She, being well-read herself, steered me towards the English, European and

American classics. Detective fiction of the English Golden Age, for which she too had a weakness, was tolerated, but the sort of popular reading permitted in most homes (comics, for example) was firmly discouraged. So I progressed from Beatrix Potter, A. A. Milne and Kenneth Grahame to Ballantyne, Blackmore and Stevenson, and then, when I was ten, to Dickens, Dumas, Hugo, Mark Twain, Poe, Jack London and Louisa M. Alcott. About this time, I was also allowed some modern authors to read. Wells, Chesterton, Steinbeck and Hemingway first came within my ken, though the titles were chosen judiciously – some were deemed 'unsuitable'. *The Red Pony*, *The Pearl*, and *Burning Bright* were allowed, but *Cannery Row* was considered a little too racy and deferred for later consumption. At the age of twelve, I first read Tolkien (*The Lord of the Rings*) and Evelyn Waugh (*The Loved One*), both Catholic authors, though I didn't know that at the time. Even after my fourteenth birthday, my mother, without any longer prescribing my reading, continued unobtrusively to influence it by choosing the books I was given for Christmas and birthday presents. And the books became more adult. That is to say, while novels such as those by Tolkien and Waugh already mentioned, can be read on more than one level, the books I was now given to read simply could not be read as just adventure stories or comedies. They were pitched unequivocally at an adult intellectual level and could not be understood in any other way. Thomas Mann's *Buddenbrooks* and *The Magic Mountain*, Hermann Hesse's *Steppenwolf* and *Narziss and Goldmund*, Alain Fournier's *Le Grand Meaulnes*, Cocteau's *Les Enfants Terribles*, Conrad's *Heart of Darkness*, Wyndham Lewis's *The Revenge for Love*, Brecht's *The*

Threepenny Novel and Peake's *Gormenghast* trilogy were among the books I read for the first time between the ages of fourteen and sixteen.

I became, and have remained ever since, an inveterate haunter of bookshops, especially second-hand bookshops. There was a good one – Hall's Bookshop – in Tunbridge Wells, a town not far from our home, where I went often. One day, I returned from a visit with a copy of Bertrand Russell's *Sceptical Essays*. On the first page, I read something like this (I quote from memory so the words may not be exact)—

'I wish to propose for the reader's favourable considera-
tion a doctrine which may, I fear, appear wildly para-
doxical and subversive. The doctrine in question is this:
that it is undesirable to believe a proposition when there
is no ground whatsoever for supposing it to be true.

'I am aware,' Russell continued mischievously, 'that
such a doctrine, if adopted, would tend to diminish the
income of bookmakers, bishops and clairvoyants....'

Well! This was heady stuff for a sixteen-year-old. The tone – urbane, witty, mocking and ironic – appealed to the youthful iconoclast in me. I had the agreeable feeling of reading something very clever, daring and sophisticated, which of course effortlessly develops into the even more agreeable feeling of being very clever, daring and sophisticated oneself. I did not immediately abandon my religious beliefs but, for the first time, I found them called seriously into question. Here was a book by an eminent philosopher, and an outstandingly clever man, who clearly did not believe in God. Why? The sceptical essays didn't answer that question to my satisfaction. Nor did another book by Russell entitled *Why I Am Not a Christian*. It included a transcript of a famous broadcast debate between Russell and Father Frederick Copleston S. J. on the existence of God. I read it and was mystified. It seemed to me then (and still seems to me now) that Copleston had much the better of the argument. Yet Russell included this in a book that sought to explain why he was not a Christian and, presumably, sought also to justify his position. I was puzzled.

Religious questions, especially the fundamental one of the existence of God, continued to play a large part in my intellectual development. I took to going on long, solitary walks and revolving the question of God's existence in my mind. It still seemed to me, on one level, a matter of common sense, but on another…why, if God existed, was there so little evidence? Why did He not answer prayers? Why was He so obstinately silent, so withdrawn, so *absent*? Why did God cause or permit some miracles (cures at Lourdes, for instance) but not others (not everyone who went to Lourdes and prayed for a cure got one)? Why did wicked people (sometimes) prosper and the innocent (sometimes) suffer? Why did natural disasters occur? Why did so many clever people not believe in Him? Why did the people who did believe in Him (Christians, Jews and Muslims) constantly fight among themselves, despite agreeing on so much? Why were so many professing Christians such poor advertisements for Christianity? In fact, why did religious believers in general fall so far short of the standards enjoined upon them by their faith? It was all very perplexing.

And then, on one of my walks, something happened. My

brother and sister had both been baptized about the age of sixteen and I was aware that I, too, should be thinking about getting baptized. But there was a problem. Like many adolescents, I was very self-conscious. Baptists practise baptism by immersion and I was frankly horrified at the thought of being 'dunked' in a public ceremony. What if something went wrong, if I slipped for instance? I would look ridiculous. I would be laughed at. So the problem was, I knew I ought to be baptized, but I very much did not want to go through with it. I wanted to find a reason for not being baptized even though I knew I ought to be baptized; in fact, as a Christian, I *had* to be baptized. And then it came to me. If my faith was not equal to this (very minor) trial, then I didn't really believe in God at all. I stopped and thought about this. I didn't believe in God. *I did not believe in God.* It seemed an enormous thing. Yet nothing happened. The skies didn't darken. No thunderbolt fell. I heard no voice warning me that I had blasphemed or apostatized. In fact, I heard no communication at all. Nothing. Not a word. That was that, then. I didn't believe in God. At first, I felt an emptiness, a hollow feeling. It seemed to me that this was a momentous decision – but what had actually changed? Anything? Nothing? I wasn't sure. But gradually, over the next days and weeks, a feeling of enormous relief came over me. I didn't have to be baptized after all. Come to think of it, I didn't have to do, or be, anything. I was free! Free to decide for myself what I wanted to do. Free to decide what was right and what was wrong according only to my own judgment and the promptings of my conscience. Free to act as I saw fit. Free to believe whatever I saw fit. From now on, I wouldn't listen to any superstitious religious nonsense. I was the captain of my soul and, for the rest of my life, I would decide things for myself.

It is now, I hope, clear why I said earlier that very few people are argued into, or out of, religious belief. I certainly wasn't. There was, you will note, nothing that could be called ratiocination – a process of reasoning – in what passed through my mind. On the contrary, I derived, quite improperly, an ontological conclusion from introspection into a mental state. I did not believe in God. Therefore God did not exist. I moved from a statement about by own mind to a statement about God. It is scarcely credible that a sane person can reason thus without being aware of the logical impropriety of doing so. Yet I did. Many do. You will also note that my loss of belief in God had the convenient consequence that I no longer had to do something I very much wanted to avoid. Religious believers are often accused of wishful thinking. The extent to which unbelief may also be the product of wishful thinking is often ignored.

Anyway, my new-found atheism (or agnosticism – I was never quite sure which more accurately designated my beliefs) seemed to me profoundly liberating. It also gave me the sensation of being on the side of the intelligent, the rational, the intellectually bold minority who dared to challenge received wisdom; who were not satisfied with the opinions of the herd; who would not follow a multitude for anything. This sensation was very gratifying. I dared to think for myself. I was independent, critical, sceptical. I, too, could be mocking, urbane and ironic. I read other volumes of Russell's essays and was overcome with admiration. The cool, elegant prose, the air of aristocratic superiority, the extreme unconventionality of the opinions, the refusal to believe anything without evidence, the contempt for religion and for all orthodoxy, the pervasive mockery of beliefs that (according to Russell) lacked a rational foundation – all this was to me delightful. I affected an ultra-rationalistic outlook, which must have seemed both ludicrous and insufferably priggish to any impartial observer. But I was mercifully unaware of how I appeared to others. Bertrand Russell was my new literary hero. From now on, I would model myself on him.

After the first shock had worn off, I didn't much regret my loss of religious faith, which rather confirms that I didn't have much faith to lose. I gave very little thought to God, or Christianity, or religion in general. Why should I? I no longer believed in them. They were fairy tales, relics of childhood, which I had now put away along with other childish things. And, from this time until I was past thirty, religion ceased altogether to feature in my reading. On the contrary, I was eager to read everything I could find by other atheists and agnostics. I wanted to explore all the exciting possibilities opened up for me by my new, Godless view of the world.

To begin with, I wanted to read everything by Bertrand Russell I could get my hands on. I found two volumes – *Philosophical Essays* and *Essays in Analysis* – in a nearby bookshop and bought them both. But my elation over my new acquisitions was short-lived. The first volume contained some essays I could understand with an effort, but the second I could make neither head nor tail of. They were technical essays on logic and, for the most part, could not have been further from my comprehension if they had been written in Sanskrit. This was a blow. I prided myself on understanding everything I read, including books that would normally be considered far too advanced for someone of my age, and finding something beyond my reach was a new and chastening experience. Clearly, I should have to be more discriminating in my choice of reading material. Not all philosophy was for everybody, and I quickly came to the conclusion that quite a lot of it was not for me. Essays in linguistic analysis, of which a number of the books I acquired second-hand seemed chiefly to consist, were dry, unappetizing fare to someone impatient to find answers to the big philosophical questions such as, How ought one to live? I bought a book called *An Atheist's Values* by Richard Robinson. This was written in clear, accessible prose that avoided technical jargon. It was both clever enough to be flattering to my vanity and simple enough to be understood. It contained one argument that both impressed and worried me. The Christian concept of God, it said, was formed by taking three propositions together, viz. God is all-powerful; God is all-benevolent; there is much suffering in the world. Now, logically, if God were all-powerful and suffering existed, He would not be all-benevolent. If God were all-benevolent and suffering existed, He would not be all-powerful. And if God were all-powerful and all-benevolent, suffering would not exist. And this, Robinson concluded triumphantly, mathematically disposes of official Christianity, although, he prudently added, that conclusion had been endlessly fought against by means of the doctrine of free will. I was impressed by the apparently inexorable logic of the argument, but worried that it seemed too pat. If the matter was as simple as that, why wasn't everyone an atheist? Or, at least, why was anyone a Christian? And Christians, I knew, included some highly intelligent people. It didn't seem likely to me that they would be unaware of this rather obvious objection to their creed or unprepared to meet it. Nonetheless, I thought it was an argument I could use in debate with Christian adversaries and I stored it away in my mind for future reference.

When I began my 'A'-level studies, my atheism received an unexpected boost. One of the set texts was Albert Camus' *L'Étranger*, which introduced me to French existentialism. I read all the novels, short stories and plays by Camus and Jean-Paul Sartre, as well as Camus' two philosophical essays, *Le Mythe de Sisyphe* and *L'Homme Révolté*. I also read Sartre's short lecture, *Existentialism and Humanism*. His major philosophical works were beyond me at that stage. Now basing one's understanding of Sartrean existentialism on the fiction, the plays, and a popular exposition of existentialist doctrine is rather like basing one's understanding of Marxism on *The Communist Manifesto*. There are no short cuts in philosophy, or in any other academically respectable discipline. My knowledge of philosophy was, and has always remained, limited and superficial: which is to say, that my knowledge of the subject is commensurate with my interest in it. The technical side of philosophy – linguistic analysis in the Anglo-Saxon school and phenomenology in the Continental[3] – had few attractions for me, and I did not pursue it.

But even with my modest grasp of philosophy, it was apparent that there was a new and (by me) previously unconsidered problem with atheism. It was not monolithic. Christians, though divided on some issues, had many beliefs in common. Even Christians, Jews and Muslims, despite their religious differences, had much on which they could agree. Indeed, they had much on which they *had* to agree, like it or not, for it was prescribed by their creed, or code, or canon. But atheists did not. They had no generally accepted creed, or code, or canon. They did not have to agree about anything except atheism and, as a matter of demonstrable fact, they disagreed about almost everything else. They ranged from Nietzsche to George Eliot, from Sartre to Russell, and from Marx to Freud. No two of them, it seemed, had any beliefs in common except atheism itself. Nietzsche's view was that rejection of the Christian metaphysic entailed rejection of Christian morality, but George Eliot, despite having abandoned all belief in the supernatural, thought that Christian morality was the noblest invention of man and ought to be retained. Sartre, following Heidegger, postulated different modes of being, being-in-itself – the brute existence of things – and being-for-itself – the free yet responsible existence of human beings, an insight he elaborated at considerable length in *L'Être et le Néant*, but Russell, in his *The Wisdom of the West*, dismissed such metaphysical speculations as being 'in the best German traditions of poetic vagueness and linguistic extravagance'. Marx thought religion was an expression of material realities and economic injustice, whereas Freud thought it was mere wish-fulfilment. This was disconcerting. It seemed that the matter was not so simple as deciding between theism and atheism. Having decided for atheism, one then had to decide what kind of atheism one believed in. Or, to put it another way, one had to decide what followed from atheism, what logical consequences a position of consistent atheism had for one's other beliefs about the world. And this was precisely what atheists could not agree on.

By the time I was nineteen, my beliefs might have been

summarized as follows. I did not believe in God. I thought, under the influence of Russell and Richard Robinson, that reason was the highest good, and, under the influence of Camus and Sartre, that man was alone and free in an absurd universe. I also thought, under the influence of Conrad, that 'the world rested on a very few ideas, notably on the idea of Fidelity', and, under the influence of Camus, that personal authenticity was the ultimate criterion of truth and goodness. I thought, under the influence of T. S. Eliot, that high culture and its preservation and transmission to future generations were all-important, and, under the influence of the then-prevailing *Zeitgeist*, that tradition (which included high culture) was an external constraint that I had to rebel against. Apart from my belief in authenticity, I had no specifically ethical ideas whatsoever. Priding myself on my independence of mind, I hadn't got an original thought in my head. Having abandoned Christian orthodoxy, I had constructed a bizarre orthodoxy of my own based on an eccentric *mélange* of ideas drawn from different and mostly incompatible sources, and cobbled together without regard for truth, consistency, coherence or even plausibility. I was in a state of the utmost confusion but didn't even realize it.

Interlude

Genes, Environment
and History

Anyone's ideas are shaped by the interactions of three things: their inherent capacities, aptitudes and tastes; their immediate environment and personal experience; and the historical and cultural context in which they live. It is worth pausing a moment to look at each of these factors.

As to my capacities, aptitudes and tastes at school, I was good at languages, literature, religious studies and history, but poor at maths and the hard sciences. I loved Latin and French. I loved reading and had an insatiable and varied appetite for literature, both prose and poetry. I also loved music, and my tastes, formed by my father's, ranged from Bach and Handel to Stravinsky and Copland. I had a special love for French and Italian opera. I had at first no interest whatever in contemporary popular music. Later, in my twenties, I developed an interest of sorts that came about in a rather unusual way. I had been listening to some mediæval troubadour songs performed by the cultivated Swiss tenor, Hugues Cuénod, and was wondering idly what the original troubadours would have sounded like. They would not have been trained in conservatories or music colleges. They would not have had classically trained voices or instruments made by great craftsmen. They were itinerant musicians.[4] Their instruments would have been rough-and-ready, probably homemade and handed down, and probably also battered and much-travelled. Their voices would have been harsh and untutored. The music they sang would have been folksongs, or derived from folksong. All of a sudden it came to me: we had an exact contemporary analogy for the troubadours – the country blues singers of the early twentieth century. From that time on, I became interested in recordings of Leadbelly, Blind Lemon Jefferson, Robert Johnson and other early bluesmen. I was amazed by the energy and intensity of their singing and playing, the raw power of their voices, their instinctive musicianship, their vividness as musical communicators. My interest in the blues led me on to explore the Chicago blues sound of Sonny Boy Williamson, Muddy Waters and Howlin' Wolf, and then on to rock bands and musicians who had been influenced by the blues: Bob Dylan, Van Morrison, Ry Cooder, Randy Newman, and Little Feat. I also became interested in British folk groups like Steeleye Span, Pentangle, Incantation and Fairport Convention, and in bands like Sky who explored the boundaries between classical music and rock. But all of this remained peripheral to my central musical interests, which were firmly anchored in the European classical tradition. All these tastes had been with me from my earliest days and are with me still. They are fundamental to my sense of identity.

Environmentally, the constants in my life were my family, books and music. Because of our peripatetic way of life, friendships, though important, were subject to sudden rupture at unpredictable intervals. I have already said that my literary education was supervised by my mother. My musical education was my father's affair. I grew up surrounded by music: Purcell, J. S. Bach and Handel; Haydn and Mozart; Beethoven and Schubert; Brahms and Wagner; Chopin and Liszt; Tchaikovsky and Dvořák; Elgar, Delius and Vaughan Williams; Mahler and Rachmaninov; Verdi and Puccini – I was introduced to all of it. My father's tastes didn't extend to early music, mainly, I suspect, because in those days there were so few opportunities to hear any. And we had nothing more modern-sounding than Stravinsky, Britten or Bartók, which may explain why, to this day, I detest the sort of music that sounds as though it were meant to be seen and not heard. Throughout my atheist years, music was my only contact with religion; yet, strangely, I didn't make the connexion. I would listen to mass settings by Haydn or Mozart or Schubert without consciously noting that this was the Catholic Mass. I would listen to settings of the *Stabat Mater* by Pergolesi or Poulenc without taking in the obvious fact that this was an extended meditation, in words and music, on the sufferings of the Mother of God at the foot of the Cross. I would listen to the Passions and the church cantatas of J. S. Bach or to Elgar's *Dream of Gerontius*, and be deeply moved by the words and the music, without consciously connecting the experience with the religious subject of the texts. I cannot account for this. It seems incredible to me now that I could have been so obtuse.[5]

As to my literary tastes, they were from the first, and have always remained, catholic with a small 'c'. Literature is a much wider field than philosophy. Anyone who reads widely in literature – by which I mean anyone who reads and studies sympathetically books of different times and different cultures; who reads poetry as well as prose; who reads in more than one language; who reads in multiple literary genres – myths, legends, fables, fairy tales, parables, scriptures, spiritual and devotional works, essays, histories, plays, novels and novellas, short stories, sermons, mediæval romances, epic and lyric poems, odes, narrative verse, satires, biographies and autobiographies, diaries and journals, volumes of letters, notebooks and commonplace books, travel literature, philosophy, theology, and scientific treatises – will become acquainted with a broader spectrum of views and ideas than someone who merely studies philosophy. The ideas may not be set out and developed systematically; the views may not be properly related to each other, and such a person's mental landscape may, in consequence, be unmapped and difficult to negotiate; but his inner resources will be incomparably richer than those of someone whose reading has been more limited, whether from choice or from lack of opportunities. His frame of reference will be wider and more comprehensive; his sympathies, more generous; his tastes, more eclectic. It is important to stress this point: in an age of increasing specialization, it is in danger of being forgotten.

The wider historical and cultural context of my life – of all our lives today – is the result of a series of intellectual movements that, individually and collectively, have had the effect of weakening the hold of Christianity on the European psyche and imagination. First, the Renaissance, with its revival of the literature and oratory of classical antiquity and the development of humanist, as opposed to scholastic, methods of inquiry and reasoning, challenged the previously unquestioned dominion of the Catholic Church in intellectual and academic matters. Then the Protestant Reformation undermined the authority of the Church in spiritual affairs. Church tradition was rejected in the name of a supposedly purer, more Biblical Christianity. Then the Enlightenment, with its enthronement of reason as the primary source of legitimacy and authority, and its belief in science and the scientific method of inquiry as the sole route to knowledge, further loosened the bonds between the Church and education. After the Enlightenment, the Romantic Movement, with its emphasis on the primacy of the individual over the collective, the will over the intellect, imagination over reason, creativity over custom, and liberty over law, instituted the ultimate rebellion: the revolt of man against God. Religion was seen as a constraint on individual freedom, an attempt to shackle and imprison the human will. Only sheep would submit tamely to such constraints. Men who aspired to transcend the condition of servitude would fight for their freedom and independence.

The modern age, consciously the heir to this history of incrementally growing insurgency against all forms of authority and spurred on by the disastrous moral, social, political and economic effects of two world wars, took the Romantic rebellion to its logical conclusion. Artistic movements such as Dadaism and Futurism, with their rejection of the past and of externally imposed meaning, and their enthusiasm for the absurd, and political movements of the extreme left such as Marxism-Leninism and anarchism, foreshadowed the counter-culture of the 1960s, which explicitly rejected all forms of authority – social, political, cultural, ecclesial and military – in the name of youth, freedom and autonomy. This personal autonomy acknowledged no bounds but presumed itself to be sovereign. It alone was the supreme good. Its authority was irrefragable.

By the late 1970s, the '60s counter-culture had yielded its fruit: a generation with no knowledge of, or interest in, culture (seen as the product of 'dead white European males') or cultural history, and with no sense of cultural or religious roots. Lacking these, the young people of this generation also lacked any notion of the historical interdependence and interpenetration of culture and religion.

Following from these developments, and from the technological revolution of the 1980s and the consequent exponential increase in entertainment / communication technology,[6] there has emerged a generation that combines a high degree of functional intelligence with a disinclination to apply that intelligence to anything except the making of money and the pursuit of trivial amusements. For them, high culture is 'boring' and 'irrelevant', art is reduced to crude entertainment (pornography, computer games, witless game shows, soap operas, reality TV, action movies), and thought to diversion. The kind of serious study and patient reflection that produces the artefacts and mentefacts of high culture – art, architecture, literature, music; systems of philosophy, law and government; works of theology and religious thought – is seldom undertaken. As the French Cardinal, Paul Poupard, has said, *homo religiosus* – man consciously made in the image of God – has given way to *homo economicus* – man as supplier and consumer – and he in turn has yielded to *homo cocacolanus* – the man who drinks Coca-Cola, a man devoid of culture, learning or intellectual aspiration of any kind. In such an age, the man of high culture, who values learning for its own sake and is naturally drawn to consider religious and philosophical questions, will become increasingly an anachronism.

Such was the background to my early life. If I had been asked, at the age of twenty-five or thirty, to explain my rationale for atheism, I would have pointed to the existence of innocent suffering and asked how that could be reconciled to the idea of an all-powerful, all-benevolent God. I would have said that the world offers no positive evidence for the existence of God and that God was merely an unnecessary hypothesis. I would have said that religion is simply untrue history or myth, and I would have agreed with Freud that its origins lie in human psychological needs. Finally, I would have echoed Sartre in regarding religion as 'bad faith', the recourse of those too weak and dishonest to accept the burden of freedom and responsibility. Yet, with hindsight, all of these seem to me rationalizations of a view I had accepted 'off the peg', partly in order to fit in better with those around me, and partly because it allowed me to think and act as I wanted to think and act, without having to worry about the constraints of an external authority, or anything so inconvenient, or so stubbornly resistant to my will, as objective truth.

The Cracks Begin
to Appear

The Problem
That Innocents Suffer

One day, when I was about thirty, I watched David Lynch's remarkable film, *The Elephant Man*. I did so not deliberately but quite idly, because nothing better was 'on' and I had nothing more diverting to do. The film interested me extremely and I immediately bought a copy of Michael Howell's and Peter Ford's authoritative account entitled *The Illustrated True History of the Elephant Man*, in order to see how far the film accorded with the facts. Included as an appendix in Howell's and Ford's book was a brief memoir of Joseph Merrick, the so-called Elephant Man, by Frederick Treves, the surgeon who treated him and who eventually secured for him accommodation at the Royal London Hospital, where he was able to spend the last three years of his life. Treves' memoir was not entirely accurate, partly it seems because Merrick did not completely confide in him, and partly because, for unexplained reasons, Treves altered some of the details. For example, he changed Merrick's Christian name from Joseph to John. Despite a few such minor discrepancies, Treves' memoir remains an important source of information about Merrick, his life and his medical condition. I found that the filmmakers had taken some liberties, but not more than were necessary to turn the extraordinary story of Joseph Carey Merrick from a factual biography into a work of cinematic art. Despite some sentimentalizing and some telescoping of timelines and events, in its substance the film was true to the facts.

And the facts were remarkable. Joseph Merrick may well have been the most hideously deformed human being who ever lived. It is thought that he probably suffered from a singularly unfortunate combination of neurofibromatosis type 1 and Proteus syndrome, which caused not only foul-smelling, fungus-like growths to appear on his skin, but also monstrous deformities of his head, face and body. These growths and deformities were so extreme that, were it not for photographic evidence, they would be scarcely credible. They made it impossible for Merrick to gain employment or to earn a living as a door-to-door salesman because his appearance horrified his prospective customers. Eventually, without any other means of securing a livelihood, he hired himself out to the proprietor of a freak show, where he was exhibited, an object of public revulsion, until the police deemed the show degrading and closed it down. Merrick was then sold to a new owner and travelled to Belgium, where the law took a more tolerant view of such entertainments. There his new owner robbed him of his savings and left him to find his way back to England as best he could. With the help of some of the other 'freaks', he was able to make his way to London, where he was found at Liverpool Street Station in a state of exhaustion bordering on collapse. Police who were summoned to the scene found, in Merrick's pocket, Frederick Treves' card. (During Merrick's time in the London freak show, he had been examined by Treves at the medical college opposite, where Treves was a lecturer on anatomy.) Treves took Merrick into his care. With the agreement of the supervising committee of the Royal London Hospital, and thanks to both royal patronage and a generous subscription from the public in response to an appeal, Treves was able to arrange accommodation for Merrick in some converted rooms in the hospital basement. There Merrick lived, cared for by the hospital staff, for the remaining three years of his life. He was visited daily by Treves and was able also to receive other visitors. He died at the age of twenty-seven, probably of a dislocation of the neck brought about by an attempt to sleep 'like normal people'.

In his memoir, Treves observes—

'those who are interested in the evolution of character might speculate as to the effect of this brutish life upon a sensitive and intelligent man [such as he had found Merrick to be – against his expectations, for he had at first taken Merrick for an imbecile: an impression facilitated by the difficulty of understanding Merrick's speech, which, owing to his facial deformities, was much impaired]. It would be reasonable to surmise that he would become a spiteful and malignant misanthrope, swollen with venom and filled with hatred of his fellow-men, or, on the other hand, that he would degenerate into a despairing melancholic on the verge of idiocy. Merrick, however, was no such being. ... He showed himself to be a gentle, affectionate and lovable creature...free from any trace of cynicism or resentment, without a grievance and without an unkind word for anyone. I have never heard him complain. I have never heard him deplore his ruined life or resent the treatment he had received. His journey in life had been indeed along a *via dolorosa*, the road had been uphill all the way, and now...he...suddenly found himself...in a friendly inn, bright with light and warm with welcome. His gratitude to those about him was pathetic in its sincerity and eloquent in the childlike simplicity with which it was expressed.'

I have quoted from Treves' memoir at some length because this passage makes a point of the greatest importance. One of the reasons I gave for disbelieving in the existence of the Christian God was that innocents suffer. But what if that reason does not satisfy the suffering innocents themselves? What if they deny that their sufferings render belief in an all-loving, all-powerful God impossible? I had always held that no one, apart from God, if He exists, can claim the right to forgive wrongs done to another. By the same token, how could I claim the right to interpret, and draw conclusions from, the sufferings of others, as if I had been empowered to act on their behalf? For my part, I had led a life made up almost entirely of comfort and privilege. My health was, and always had been, good. I had never broken a bone or undergone surgery. I had never required medical treatment for a serious condition. I was as nearly without personal experience of suffering as any human being who has ever walked the earth. By what right could I judge what was an appropriate response to sufferings, of which I had no experience, no direct knowledge, of which indeed I could not even form a remotely adequate conception? Joseph Merrick's sufferings, physical and mental, were extreme. It is hard to conceive of anything worse than the fate of being rejected, abhorred and despised by almost the entire human race, and such was Merrick's lot until Treves rescued him from destitution and the streets. Yet Merrick was neither bitter nor melancholic. On the contrary, he was, on Treves' testimony, 'gentle, affectionate and lovable'. And, strangest of all, he was a devout Christian, with an intimate knowledge of the Bible and the Book of Common Prayer.

This surprised – even shocked – me. But still, Joseph Merrick was only one person. A single instance of anything proves only that there are aberrations; that the rule admits of exceptions. It would be wrong to draw a general conclusion from a single case. And anyway, I was by no means sure what conclusion I should draw, even from multiple cases of this kind. Not that I knew of any others. Not then.

But that was about to change.

I had always enjoyed American literature, especially the Southern writers. Faulkner, Thomas Wolfe, Carson McCullers and Eudora Welty were among my enthusiasms. So it was inevitable that I would one day encounter the works of Flannery O'Connor. The first thing of hers I read was her second novel, a short work called *The Violent Bear It Away*. It hit me like a thunderbolt out of a clear blue sky. I had no idea what to make of it. However, it was clear that this was a highly original work by an important writer. I still did not realize exactly how important she would become for me, but I read everything else by her I could find. Quantitatively, there didn't seem to be much – just one other novel, *Wise Blood*, also quite short, and two collections of short stories – but everything had this same visionary quality. She was, I realized, a Catholic, which made her unusual among the Southern writers, and accounted to some extent for her strange, oblique 'take' on the world. Her style was deceptively simple. She had the ability to convey complex ideas in simple terms, using deliberately spare prose and a carefully pared down vocabulary. To anyone inured to purely secular ways of thinking and to a materialist philosophy, she appeared like a prophet gate-crashing a cocktail party – enigmatic, shocking, challenging, and fascinating.

Having exhausted the fiction, I discovered that O'Connor's only other published works were a slim volume of essays and lectures entitled *Mystery and Manners* and a substantial selection of her letters which had been edited by her friends, Sally and Robert Fitzgerald, and published after her death under the intriguing title *The Habit of Being.* I bought both. *Mystery and Manners* included a piece called 'Introduction to a Memoir of Mary Ann'. Though little more than twenty pages long, it was a revelation. O'Connor took three apparently unrelated themes – the life of a little, terminally ill American girl, the writings of Nathaniel Hawthorne, and the work of Hawthorne's daughter, Rose – wove them together in an intricate counterpoint as dazzling in its technical virtuosity as the finale of Mozart's 'Jupiter' Symphony, and concluded with a magnificent meditation on the meaning of the communion of saints. But it was not the virtuosity of the writing, remarkable though that was, that stayed in the memory. As ever with O'Connor, or with any great artist, technique is simply a means to an end. And the end was to introduce to the reading public a life that exemplified what O'Connor meant when, in reply to a questioner who asked her why she wrote so often about grotesques, she said, 'For the hard of hearing, you have to shout. And for the almost blind, you draw large, startling pictures.' Mary Ann, like Joseph Merrick, was such a picture.

Mary Ann Long was a little girl who had been born with a cancerous tumour on the side of her face, which necessitated the removal of one eye. From the age of three until her death nine years later, she lived in the care of Dominican nuns at Our Lady of Perpetual Help Free Cancer Home in Atlanta, Georgia. When the nuns originally wrote to O'Connor, they enclosed a photograph. O'Connor writes—

'I had glanced at it when I first opened the letter, and had put it quickly aside. Now I picked it up to give it a last cursory look before returning it to the Sisters. It showed a little girl in her First Communion dress and veil. She was sitting on a bench, holding something I could not make out. Her small face was straight and bright on one side. The other side was protuberant, the eye was bandaged, the nose and mouth crowded slightly out of place. The child looked out at her observer with an obvious happiness and composure. I continued to gaze at the picture long after I had thought to be finished with it.'

The nuns were convinced that the story of this little girl, who had brightened the lives of all who came into contact with her, was a truly remarkable one and ought to be told – and who better to tell it than a well-known Catholic novelist? O'Connor, understandably appalled at this request, artfully suggested that the nuns themselves, who after all had known Mary Ann, should write her story, whereupon she would gladly write an introduction that could be published with it. She had no doubt that this was safe generosity. She did not expect to hear from them again. But, of course, she did; and that was how the introduction came to be written.

At one point in the introduction, O'Connor says—

'She [Mary Ann] and the Sisters who had taught her had fashioned from her unfinished face the material of her death. The creative action of the Christian's life is to prepare his death in Christ. It is a continuous action in which this world's goods are utilized to the fullest, both positive gifts and what Père Teilhard de Chardin calls "passive diminishments". Mary Ann's diminishment was extreme, but she was equipped by natural intelligence and by a suitable education, not simply to endure it, but to build upon it. She was an extraordinarily rich little girl.'

An extraordinarily rich little girl? Hardly the first words that would come to mind to describe a child born with an incurable cancer. Yet Mary Ann herself would probably have agreed. Her condition did not prevent her from enjoying life, having friends, being happy, not envying others. All the same, does anyone else have the right to say of a child so grievously afflicted that she was 'an extraordinarily rich little girl'? Easy for you to say, might be the retort.

But it wasn't easy for O'Connor to say. She herself had inherited a fatal disease, disseminated lupus, from her father, and died of it when she was thirty-nine. For much of her short life, she was an invalid, often in great pain, and living under what she knew to be a death sentence. She had been devastated when her father had died of lupus when she was fifteen. Her own diagnosis was pronounced just ten years later. When it came to suffering, physical and mental, Flannery O'Connor knew what she was talking about. Yet, in the 600-odd pages of her letters, I found not one word of self-pity or complaint. Her attitude to her illness could best be described as matter-of-fact. What I did find in those letters in abundance was wisdom and a sense of eremitic detachment from the world, together with wit, gaiety, sardonic humour, seriousness and high intelligence. She and Mary Ann, then, were two more cases of suffering innocents who did not – and saw no reason to – use their suffering to argue against the existence of God. O'Connor herself has this to say on the subject—

'One of the tendencies of our age is to use the suffering of children to discredit the goodness of God, and once you have discredited his goodness, you are done with him. The Alymers whom Hawthorne saw as a menace have multiplied. Busy cutting down human imperfection, they are making headway also on the raw material of the good. Ivan Karamazov cannot believe as long as one child is in torment; Camus' hero cannot accept the divinity of Christ because of the massacre of the innocents. In this popular pity, we mark our gain in sensibility and our loss in vision. If other ages felt less, they saw more, even if they saw with the blind, prophetical, unsentimental eye of acceptance, which is to say, of faith. In the absence of this faith now, we govern by tenderness. It is a tenderness which, long since cut off from the person of Christ, is wrapped in theory. When tenderness is detached from the source of tenderness, its logical outcome is terror. It ends in forced-labor camps and in the fumes of the gas chamber.'

That unforgettable passage seemed to me, when I first read it, the most radical challenge to the atheistic argument from innocent suffering since the Book of Job. It seems so still.[7]

None of this means that the suffering of innocents is not a problem for Christianity. But it does suggest that the problem may be something less than the insuperable obstacle that some of Christianity's secular critics assume it to be. Why innocents suffer is a mystery. To some extent it will always remain so. But, as I later discovered, it was not a subject that Christian writers had shirked, or one on which they had retreated into an embarrassed silence.

The World Offers no Positive
Evidence for the Existence of God

ONE POINT MUST be clarified at the outset: the term 'positive' in this context is to be understood as the opposite to 'negative', not as the opposite to 'uncertain'.

This was the second of my reasons for being an atheist. But was it true? At any rate, it was a large claim, not least because any one person's knowledge of the world is very limited. The claim that the world offers no positive evidence for the existence of God seems to imply that the person making the claim has experienced, or personally scrutinized, everything that the world has to offer. Minimally, it requires that the person making the claim should be acquainted with everything that the world has to offer, although that acquaintance may rely to a certain extent on second-hand knowledge derived from trustworthy authorities. But even if the claim is taken at its weakest, it should be obvious that it is one that no one can properly make.

Consider what is involved. Many people, for example, claim to have undergone religious experience. Now it may be that I am not such a person. But that does not give me the right to dismiss other people's accounts of their experience. I cannot reasonably claim that, because I have never had, say, a mystical experience, mystical experiences are invalid, or impossible, and that those who claim to have had such experiences are insane, deluded or lying. Similarly, some interpret the highest aesthetic experiences as indicative of God's existence; that is, they consider that, while such experiences do not prove that God exists, they point to His existence as the most probable explanation of certain features of reality. This has been amusingly encapsulated in the 'argument', 'There is the music of Johann Sebastian Bach. Therefore God exists.' Clearly, that argument is not valid if it is viewed as an attempt to prove God's existence deductively. But if it is viewed merely as a claim that Bach's music is, as it were, a signpost pointing to God's existence as a rational explanation, perhaps even the *most* rational explanation, of a phenomenon otherwise very difficult, if not impossible, to account for, it is not without merit.

What other features of the world might be regarded as indicative of God's existence? In fact, quite a few. For example: the existence of anything rather than nothing; the existence of life; the existence of consciousness; the existence of self-consciousness; the existence of rational beings; the principle of causality; the general reliability of human reasoning, sensory perception, and the moral deliverances of conscience; human creativity, especially artistic creation, the acts in which we humans, by becoming creators ourselves, most obviously resemble God; natural law; natural and aesthetic beauty; the fact that the universe is apparently 'fine-tuned' to support life; the appearance of regularity, order and pattern in the universe; the existence in the human world of such concepts as love (in all its manifestations, whether as *eros*, *philia*, *storge* or *agape*), fidelity, wisdom, truth, justice, honour, duty and virtue; and the fact that all these things, and many others, are typically experienced by human beings as *gifts*, unearned benefactions for which the proper response is *gratitude.*

Again, none of these features is probative. Even in the aggregate, they fall far short of an indisputable proof. But, like religious experience, they point to the existence of God as the most probable of all the possible explanations. Certainly, they make the claim we started with – that the world offers no positive evidence for the existence of God – considerably less credible than it seemed at first sight.

Religion is Simply Untrue History or Myth

IT GOES WITHOUT saying that some of the content of all religions is myth. In the case of Christianity, the creation narratives in Genesis, for instance, are myths. But only a careless and superficial thinker would infer, from that fact, either that all religion was simply myth, or that any particular religion was entirely mythical.

Unfortunately, during the twentieth century, that view was lent an undeserved credibility from within Christianity. Theologians such as Rudolf Bultmann sought to 'demythologize' the New Testament by purging it of all supernatural elements and retaining only what was consistent with modern secular views. The word 'demythologize' is a question-begging term. It assumes, without adducing the slightest evidence, that anything in the Gospel accounts that conflicts with the modern, scientific and secular worldview, did not happen. All such elements – miracles, the Resurrection, the Transfiguration: in short, anything that required the operation of a supernatural agency – were, on this view, inventions of the evangelists, or, more simply, myths.

But this will not do. Myth is a literary genre, which, like other such genres (the novel, say, or the epic), displays certain well-known and definite characteristics. The Gospels, however, do not possess those characteristics. For example, one of the defining characteristics of myths is that they are set in times of remote but unspecified antiquity and in unspecified but vaguely indicated locations. Yet we know from the Gospels precisely when and where Jesus was born, when and where he lived, and when and where he died. The date of his birth is fixed by a very prosaic detail: that it was in the year in which Caesar Augustus instituted a census for the purpose of determining a scheme of taxation. Jesus was crucified when Pontius Pilate, an otherwise minor and unmemorable Roman official, was Proconsul in Judæa. The Gospel narratives have certain other features that distinguish them clearly from myths. One of these is the inclusion of realistic details. To cite just one example, in the story of the woman taken in adultery, it is recorded that Jesus was squatting on the ground writing with his finger in the dust. This detail adds nothing to the narrative. So why is it included? Evidently because it happened. Either the narrator was there, or he had the story from someone else who was; that witness, whether the narrator or another, saw it and recorded it because it was his purpose to record as accurately as possible all that he remembered, or could ascertain, of Jesus's life and teaching.

Such details in the Gospels are so numerous that they admit of only two possible explanations: either the evangelists were recording, as accurately as possible, their exact recollections of what they had seen, and what actually happened; or they invented the descriptive techniques and narrative method of realistic fiction eighteen hundred years before anyone else. I leave it to the reader to decide which of these explanations is the more plausible.

And there is another obvious reason why 'demythologizing' the Gospels simply won't wash. It is this: why, if the evangelists lied about the miracles and the empty tomb of Christ, should we believe them about anything else? If the only thing you know about a supposedly authoritative source is that it is unreliable, its claim to authority is destroyed. If all four of the evangelists were liars (itself a wildly implausible thesis since it both requires collusion between them and raises the question why none of their Jewish or pagan contemporaries controverted their accounts), then Christianity is without a rational foundation. You cannot have it both ways: the evangelists either are, or are not, credible witnesses. It is absurd to claim that they are credible, but only for some of the time.

The Origins of Religion
Lie in Human Psychological Needs

THIS STATEMENT CONTAINS a truth that no theist would wish to dispute – namely, that there is a deep psychological need for God in human beings. Indeed, C. S. Lewis used this to construct an ingenious philosophical argument for God's existence. The argument runs as follows: Every human longing finds fulfilment in a real object: thus hunger is satisfied by food; thirst by water; the sex drive by conjugal love. Yet human beings long for something that nothing in the world can satisfy. Therefore human beings were created for another world in which that desire will find satisfaction. That which satisfies that desire we call God.

Of course, this argument is open to the same objection as other philosophical arguments that purport to prove the existence of God – viz. that it is a *petitio*. The first premiss would certainly be challenged by atheists. Even the view that human beings long for something that nothing in the world can satisfy might be questioned, although most reflective people would probably agree with it. But that is not to the point. What is very much to the point is the fact that there is no logical step by which one can get from the human need for God to the conclusion that that need caused human beings to invent God. The need might just as easily point to the actual existence of God, as C. S. Lewis suggested. It is just as plausible to suppose that God has implanted that need in every human soul as to suppose that human beings invented God to satisfy their psychological needs. Neither hypothesis can be confirmed or disproved by empirical evidence.

Did I feel a psychological need for God? I had done without Him for fifteen years – and done pretty well, in my own estimation. I did not consciously give Him much thought. Because I disbelieved in His existence, I never prayed, never read scripture, never attended a church service, and never received a sacrament. My interest in philosophy was confined to atheistic or agnostic philosophers: religious philosophy I simply ignored. And yet...and yet. I was never able to convince myself that religion didn't matter. I somehow knew that the things religion was concerned with, the questions it raised and the answers it offered, even though I didn't believe them, were important. I respected people who were religious and who acted, or tried to act, on the principles they professed. I hated to hear such people disparaged, especially by those like me who had never lifted a finger to benefit anyone but themselves. On one occasion, I either heard or read a vicious and spiteful attack on Mother Teresa of Calcutta by the feminist, Germaine Greer, and reacted as angrily as if I had been personally insulted. And, as time went on and I became better acquainted with secular philosophy, I found it dryer, less satisfying, less capable of proposing credible answers to the urgent questions that most naturally occurred to me. It was as if I needed red meat and was being offered not even good honest vegetables, but dry straw instead.

There is a psychological need for God deep within most

human beings. But it does not follow that this need accounts for religious beliefs, still less that religious beliefs are untrue. After all, it would be equally easy to argue that there is a human psychological need for autonomy and independence, and that this accounts for the rejection of religious belief. In neither case can arguments from psychological needs lead to valid ontological conclusions.

Religion is 'Bad Faith'

THIS IS THE Sartrean view that religion is simply a prop used by those who are too weak and dishonest to face up to the burdens of freedom and responsibility. This view, of course, is attractive to those who wish to find reasons for approving of atheism. Anything that enables one, with a clear conscience, to regard theists with contempt – as hypocrites, say, or as moral weaklings – has an obvious practical utility to those who are trying to make the case for atheism. And I made full use of it.

But did it stand up to an impartial examination? After all, theists included saints, many of whom had displayed immense courage, and martyrs: not much sign there of moral weakness or reluctance to accept responsibility. Even without looking to such exalted examples, there were many instances of moral and physical courage on the part of Christians. Some had defied the Nazis or the Communists at enormous personal risk. Others had risked torture and death to work as missionaries or to smuggle bibles into countries where they were forbidden. Some voluntarily worked in leper colonies, or slums, or ill-equipped hospitals in the Third World, bringing what comfort and dignity they could to the incurably sick and the dying, despite the appalling dangers. Throughout the world, there were priests and religious working among the poor, the destitute, and the sick. Nor was this a modern phenomenon. During the Black Death in Europe, the toll among the clergy was disproportionately high, many times higher than that of the general population. The reason? The clergy were the only people who were prepared to risk their own lives by visiting the sick and the dying.

The more I looked at the evidence, rather than adopting a doctrinaire view because it suited my purpose to do so, the more it seemed to me that the Sartrean view was not just untenable, it was preposterous. It was the diametric opposite to the truth. Whether the Christian religion was true or false, the best of those who believed it seemed better and stronger characters than the best of those who did not. They seemed more self-denying, more capable of standing up to oppressors, more truthful, more courageous, and much less self-serving in their actions and their beliefs. In contrast, if there were any atheist saints or martyrs, I did not know of them. Neither, it seemed, did anyone else, for I tried hard enough to find documentary evidence of unbelievers who had displayed comparable goodness and courage in the face of the most terrible adversity. Yet, for all my endeavours, I found nothing. No martyrs who willingly gave up their lives for the truth, no saints whose lives exhibited heroic virtue. At one time, I thought that the first revolutionaries in Russia might be my atheist martyrs. But no; for they did not die for the truth, or even for what they thought was the truth. They died in a struggle for political power. They were casualties of war. After years of diligent searching, I had to accept that there were neither atheist martyrs, nor saints. This, for an atheist, was a bitter pill to swallow.

The Cracks Widen

These reflections did not immediately cause me to change my views, but they gave me reasons, in Graham Greene's words, 'to doubt my unbelief'. I was no longer as certain as I had been that God did not exist. By the time I was thirty-one, my position was much more agnostic than atheistic, although I still maintained that there was not enough evidence of God's existence to warrant any form of theistic belief.

Nevertheless, the cracks in my beliefs noted above were imperceptibly growing wider. I began to notice inconsistencies in the beliefs I held about the world. I thought that the universe was, in the existentialist sense, absurd; but I admired works of art that were nothing but attempts to discover order, pattern and meaning in the world – all of them things that, on my account of the world, did not exist. I thought that right and wrong, good and evil, were human inventions; but, when I examined my own experience, I found that I did not consider myself free to decide what was good and what evil, what was right and what wrong, but rather felt bound by a moral law that I had not invented. I thus found that, on my view of the world, there was a radical disjunction between truth and goodness. If what I believed to be true was in fact true, then goodness had no objective reality. Yet I could make no sense whatsoever of the notion of the good as purely subjective; of values, whether moral or aesthetic, as an affair of purely private judgment. If they were, on what grounds could I condemn an honest Nazi? On the grounds that my opinion differed from his? That hardly seemed sufficient. It would be rating one's opinions at a very high price to condemn a man to death on the strength of them. Yet, like most people, I thought that at least some of the Nazis were war criminals who had justly been executed at the end of the Second World War. It was clear to me that values were objective, that they existed as a fact in the world independent of what I, or anyone else, thought. I was not free, and neither was anyone else, to decide for myself that cowardice was better than courage, or cruelty than kindness; or, for that matter, that Mascagni was better than Mozart, or Shaw than Shakespeare. But the nagging problem remained: how could these views be objectively true, if, as I also believed, values were human inventions? This was more than a crack. It was a yawning chasm of inconsistency in my supposedly rational view of the world.

Strangely, the intellectual confusion I was experiencing in these years did not prevent me from functioning normally in my ordinary, day-to-day existence. I worked, ate, and slept; enjoyed visits to the theatre, the opera and concerts; went to the pub; watched sport live and on television; read books, listened to music on the radio or on recordings; wrote poetry (badly) and prose (not well, but better than poetry); in short, did everything that other people did, and did it (more or less) as well as they did. But I was conscious, all the same, that the ground was shifting underneath my feet. I knew that something would have to give. I just didn't know what. Or when. I may have given the impression that this process was quicker than it was. Actually, it was grindingly slow. It took years, if not decades. And the next impetus came from an unexpected quarter.

I had been attending concerts regularly from the age of nine and operas from the age of thirteen. By the time I was forty-four, I had been to a number of concerts impossible to calculate and to some ninety or so operas, many of which I had seen more than once. So there was nothing unusual, I thought, on the night I went to the London Coliseum to see the English National Opera's production of Poulenc's *Dialogues des Carmélites*. I didn't know the work. Essentially, as I later found out, it tells the story of the Martyrs of Compiègne, sixteen Carmelite nuns who were guillotined on the 17th July 1794 for the heinous crimes of refusing to break their vows, leave their convent and adopt civilian dress. Thousands of people died on the guillotine during the Reign of Terror. Why, out of all those people, should sixteen nuns be remembered today?

The reasons are complex and, in part, mysterious. What is certain is that the Martyrs of Compiègne have inspired a remarkable literature and historiography. Why this should be so, when others went to their deaths anonymously and were quickly forgotten, is unclear. It seems that there was an early eyewitness account of the nuns' deaths, which, many years later, having been found by chance in a second-hand bookshop by the great German Catholic writer, Gertrud von Le Fort, inspired her to write a novella, *Die Letzte am Schafott* (*The Last on the Scaffold*). This, in turn, came to the attention of a great French writer, Georges Bernanos, who fashioned out of it a remarkable play, *Dialogues des Carmélites*. Both writers allowed themselves a degree of poetic licence, inventing characters based on themselves[8] and imagining scenes, dialogue, feelings, thoughts, and so on, without tampering with the basic facts. Poulenc read Bernanos' play, was captivated, and immediately set to work on an opera based on it. So, out of one historical event, which might easily have passed unnoticed amid all the other horrors of that time and place, emerged three masterly works of art: a novella, a drama, and an opera.

I had, as I have said, seen many operas, and many more performances. Sometimes love of art has an unexpected consequence. In my case, precisely because of my love of opera, I am very rarely moved by an operatic performance. My approach to musical performance is too dry and intellectual to permit a purely emotional response. I am too absorbed by the singing and the playing, by all the technical and interpretative details, to become caught up in the action. I have been to performances of sentimental operas, such as *La Bohème* or *Madame Butterfly*, where there hasn't been a dry eye in the house except mine: I have felt nothing except delight or disappointment with the vocal or orchestral execution. To some, this seems heartless, but I can no more help it than they can help feeling moved in the way they do. For better or worse, our emotions are not at our beck and call; they cannot be summoned to order. So, when I took my seat in the Coliseum that evening, I hoped to hear a good, perhaps even (if I was lucky) a great, performance of an interesting and unfamiliar work. I hoped that the work might turn out to be one I would want to hear again. I hoped that the production would complement the words and music – or, at any rate, not interfere too much with my appreciation of them. Beyond that,

I had neither hopes nor expectations. I was totally unprepared for what followed.

Most artistic performances are routine. This is not said disparagingly, for the routine standard among good artists is very high indeed – quite high enough to give unqualified pleasure to the audience. After all, actors, singers and musicians are all trained professionals who know their job and take a pride in doing it well. So, to say of a performance by such people that it was routine, should be counted as praise, not criticism. Only the most jaundiced critic takes a poor view of a routine performance. The rest of us, whose appetites have not been sated nor tastes jaded by excessive consumption, are grateful for it. Nevertheless, occasionally a performance takes fire. Something happens – something unforeseen that cannot be willed into being – and the result is a performance of blazing intensity and shattering conviction. This was such an occasion. What caused it, no one can say. Perhaps it had something to do with that wonderful artist, Josephine Barstow, who was singing the part of Mère Marie, and whose name in a cast list was, I knew from long experience, a guarantee of something exceptional. But, on this evening, everything coalesced into something that no longer seemed to be a performance. It was as if the Old Prioress really was dying of cancer; as if Blanche de la Force's fear of the revolutionaries was actual, not feigned; as if the Reign of Terror was a palpable fact today, not an historical fact conjured up for us by a theatrical illusion that required a willing suspension of disbelief on our part.

The opera ends with the sixteen nuns singing the 'Salve Regina', the Marian hymn that is traditionally sung at the death bed of a religious, as they go, one by one, to their death on the guillotine. Poulenc's setting of this is one of the most magnificent things in the opera – or in any opera. The haunting music is punctuated by the chilling sound of the guillotine falling, again and again, as the voices dwindle in number, until only Blanche is left, singing the four last lines of the 'Veni creator spiritus'. Then the guillotine falls for the last time. The orchestra plays, very quietly, a rising phrase, repeats it. Then a single quiet chord. The curtain slowly falls. Then nothing. Silence. That night, the silence in the Coliseum was absolute. Two thousand souls sat in that immense auditorium, the second largest in London, without a sound, as if stunned. Then, haltingly, the applause started. The ovation was not tumultuous. But then *Dialogues des Carmélites* is not that kind of opera. A clamorous ovation would have been, to say the least, an inapt response to so powerful a work, especially in such an incandescent performance.

But what was I to make of this? What did it mean? Something? Nothing? Whatever I decided it should mean? Was it just an emotional experience, on a par with someone being moved by a sentimental novel or film? Hardly: because the story of the Martyrs of Compiègne, notwithstanding the modifications introduced by Le Fort and Bernanos (for which authorial licence could certainly be claimed), was substantially true, a matter of known historical fact. Was it a religious experience, then? But, if so, of what kind? What inferences, if any, could I draw from it? Were emotional and religious experiences mutually exclusive? Or could a given experience be both emotional and religious at the same time? Obviously a work of art, such as a novel, a play or an opera, cannot prove anything. But then why did they sometimes carry such persuasive force? Because they displayed truth ostensively? Or because they manipulated feelings? What was one supposed to learn from experiences? How did one go about eliciting lessons from mere happenings that, by their nature, could not be exactly repeated? Yet it seemed to me that there was a sense in which a work of art demanded an interpretative effort on the part of the viewer or listener; and that interpretations could be more or less adequate, more or less just, more or less true. For example, a casual and superficial reader might consider Dostoievsky's *Crime and Punishment* a mere thriller – and a defective one in that the plot is often interrupted by lengthy philosophical dialogues and disquisitions. However, that interpretation would manifestly fail to do justice to the philosophical, religious and psychological complexity of the novel. Now, to say that some interpretations 'do justice' to works of art more than others implies that some interpretations are more credible, more valid, truer to the facts, than others. There are many respects in which human beings differ from other species. The distinctively human need truthfully to interpret, and draw lessons from, experience is one of them. Did this experience point, as it were, beyond itself, to something else? If so, to what did it point? And how could I know?

I could not answer these questions. But the mere fact that they arose meant that, in the years from thirty to forty-four, I gradually became more and more dissatisfied with my atheistic worldview, more and more aware of its inadequacies, its incompleteness, its inability to account in any credible way for huge swathes of human experience, including those experiences that seemed the most significant, the most revelatory, to the experiencing, thinking, reflecting subject. Of course, emotional responses to stimuli, no matter how profound, how authentic, how deeply felt they may be, do not – in the nature of things, cannot – prove anything. Proof is rational and cognitive: the emotions belong to quite another sphere of mental activity. Nevertheless, we have emotions for a reason. They have no probative value, but they may, like some of the other features noted above, have an indicative value. They may serve to point our rational and cognitive faculties in a particular direction: and, according as the emotions are good (e.g. *agape*, compassion) or bad (e.g. envy, jealousy, anger), that direction may be either the right or a wrong one.

Interlude

Interlude

Friends and Teachers

W hat makes us what we are? I said earlier that our ideas are shaped by the interactions of three things: our inherent capacities, aptitudes and tastes; our immediate environment and personal experience; and the historical and cultural context in which we live. And this is true as a generalization. But what has made me the exact person I am today? Could I be different if I chose to be? If so, in what way? Clearly there are limits to choice. I could not, for example, choose to be a good enough cricketer to open the batting for England. I could not choose to be a great tenor or a virtuoso violinist. I could not choose to be an outstanding, or even a competent, mathematician. But I could, if I wanted to, choose to brush up my Latin so that I could read Virgil fluently in the original. I could probably (though this is less certain) choose to learn Russian well enough to read Dostoievsky in the original. To some extent, such choices determine the person one becomes. But before one reaches the point of being able to exercise conscious choice, one exists as a conscious human subject. And much of what has made one this particular subject, rather than another that one might have been in slightly different circumstances, is (or seems to be) chance.

Let me give an instance of what I mean. When my father was a boy, he had a friend called Jimmy Pickering. Jimmy came, like my father, from a working-class background in industrial Lancashire. It was he who introduced my father to classical music, for Jimmy had an intelligent interest in music. His parents had a radio and a gramophone and Jimmy used to save his pocket money and anything he earned to buy records. My father, who had little or no opportunity of hearing serious music at home, remembered listening with Jimmy to the Adagietto from Mahler's Fifth Symphony and even to some excerpts from Alban Berg's opera, *Wozzeck* – advanced stuff in those days. There was much else. Under Jimmy's influence, he joined the church choir and they later sang together in works such as Dvořák's *Stabat Mater*, an ambitious undertaking, one would have thought, for any church choir, however good it may have been.

Jimmy Pickering died of tuberculosis at the age of twenty. I often think of him and wonder how different my life would have been had it not been for this boy, who died some eighteen years before I was born. To him my father owed his love of music, and to my father I owe mine. Such debts can never be repaid.

Again, my mother taught me to read and, as I have said, formed my early tastes. But suppose her own tastes and aptitudes had inclined her towards mathematics rather than literature. Under her tutelage, would I have become proficient in mathematics? Would I ever have acquired, on my own without her influence, a taste for literature? Would my later interests have been in the sciences rather than the arts? Who can say?

I was singularly fortunate in my family. They fostered, and helped me to develop, the aptitudes I had, and forgave me for my shortcomings. At critical periods of my life, I have been equally fortunate in my friends and in my teachers. At my prep school in Southport, my gift for languages was recognized and encouraged. My teachers succeeded in taking me through two years of Latin and French in two terms. Starting behind the other boys, I finished ahead of them. My love of music was also encouraged, and the headmaster, in an act of characteristic kindness and generosity, revised my timetable so that I was able to attend weekly concerts, during the season at the Atkinson Art Gallery, with the senior boys. In languages, musical appreciation and literature, I had no equals in that school (nor have I had any in the seven other schools I have attended at various times in Britain, Singapore and the United States). I say this not as a boast, but in gratitude. Conversely, in mathematics I was a dunce, and, sadly, remained one for the duration of my educational career and beyond. Mathematics and the hard sciences have been as closed books to me from then on.

Later, when I was between the ages of fourteen and nineteen, three teachers exercised a decisive influence on me, and all went on to become lifelong friends. Reg Mathews taught me English language and literature, and introduced me to Shakespeare, the Restoration playwrights, and English narrative verse, and also to chamber music of which I had previously heard little. Reg, who had been an actor before he became a teacher and was a fine reader of poetry and prose, taught me how to hear poetry as well as read it. I spent many enjoyable hours in his company, walking in the Kent and Sussex countryside, or listening to recordings of poetry, drama or music. Reg's musical predilections favoured chamber music, and he introduced me to a great deal of it, including the Schubert piano trios and the great C major string quintet, the Brahms clarinet quintet and the horn trio, the rarely heard piano quintet by Borodin, and the delightful chamber works of Dvořák. Leo Conney taught me French and history and introduced me to the glories of French literature. Under Leo's guidance, I first read Camus, Sartre, Gide, Mauriac, Bloy, Mérimée, Anouilh, Bernanos, Alain-Fournier, Montherlant, Balzac, Péguy, Duhamel, Julien Green, and many others. It was Leo too who introduced me to the story of the worker priests in France, a fascinating and important chapter in the history of modern Catholicism. It is probably due to his influence that my Catholicism has a distinctly left-wing political bias to this day. Finally, Father Kevin Pelham taught me Latin and religious knowledge. My Latin, alas, was rusty from long desuetude, but, from Father Kevin's patient instruction, I learned much about the New Testament and something of the rational, disciplined approach to religious studies that is natural to the Catholic mind. It was no fault of his that it took a further thirty years for the lessons to sink in.

Reg had converted to Catholicism immediately before he was called up for military service during the Second World War, but Leo and Father Kevin were cradle Catholics. None of them made any attempt to convert me, by either force or persuasion, but their example was influential in the sense that it ensured that any aversion I then felt from Catholic doctrine and practices never extended to Catholics themselves.

Of course, I also had many friends who were not Catholics, some of whom shared my aversion from the Church, though for different reasons. Some were strong supporters of 'women's right to choose' – in other words, of abortion on demand. I supported abortion in cases where the pregnancy was the result of rape or incest, but was less convinced that it ought to be permitted in other cases. I never saw it as a valid alternative to contraception. The Church's opposition to contraception in principle, regardless of circumstances, was another stance with which many, including me, disagreed. In fact, the Church's teaching on sex generally needed, I thought, a drastic revision to bring it up to date. Most of my friends agreed that regarding masturbation as sinful, homosexuality as an objective disorder, or sex outside marriage as intrinsically wrong, were attitudes that could not be justified in the modern age and would have to be jettisoned if the Church was to survive (not that we cared whether it survived or not: in fact, on balance, we thought it would be better if it didn't). Yet, curiously, some of the friends who professed these beliefs also claimed to be Christians. True, they were not churchgoers; they didn't pray, read scripture, receive sacraments, study religion, or even believe most of what Christianity had traditionally taught and upheld. But they thought that you ought to be decent to other people and perhaps turn the other cheek – well, sometimes – and that you shouldn't steal, or murder, or sleep with someone else's wife or girlfriend (at least, not if you were likely to get found out) – and…that was enough, wasn't it? After all, God's supposed to be loving and forgiving and all that – surely he understands that we can't all be plaster saints and won't mind the odd lapse!

So chance or providence or whatever it was had thrown me in with Catholics and non-Catholics, with Christians and atheists. It had shown me that some people who called themselves Christians didn't believe what Christians have historically believed, and didn't seem to think that mattered. Did it matter? I didn't know. I thought it would be more honest, if you didn't believe what Christians had historically believed, to call yourself something else – perhaps a humanist, or an atheist, or an agnostic. Chance or providence or whatever it was had allowed me to see at close quarters the effects of different beliefs for better or worse – their effects in terms of both the actions they promoted, and the moral character of those who held them. It allowed me to see that those who grounded their moral beliefs in views about metaphysical facts had a surer and more secure foundation for such beliefs than those for whom morals were merely, in Newman's words, 'a taste and a sentiment'.

In any life, friendships are of vital importance. Not only are they life-enhancing in themselves, but they are often the chief means by which one develops intellectually, socially, morally and spiritually. The apparent accident of one's friendships, their nature and duration, may determine the direction and extent of one's moral and spiritual development. St Peter might have remained all his life a humble fisherman, generous, impetuous, impulsive, but morally frail, cowardly, weak in faith and susceptible to temptation. His friendship with Christ transformed him into a martyr willing to endure the agony of crucifixion for his Lord. Many, including some of the greatest figures in Christian history, have been led to Christ at least in part through friendships. Now, one can, of course, choose to see one's personal history as accidental, meaningless, the product of blind chance. Alternatively, one can choose to see in one's own experiences tokens of God's purposes and providence. One can discern, in the critical events and encounters of one's life, signs, opportunities, and tests: signs of God's intentions for oneself; opportunities to choose good over evil, or to apprehend God's will more clearly; tests of one's character, mettle and commitment. But one of these ways of seeing and interpreting experience must correspond to the facts more closely than the other. They may both be false, but cannot both be true. My problem, at the age of forty, was that I didn't know which was false and which, if either, was true. Worse, I didn't know what test or standard I could apply in order to find out.

The Cracks Split Wide Open

I had now reached the age of forty-four and my position might be summarized as follows. I had been raised as a Protestant. About the age of sixteen, I had lost – or, rather, abandoned – my faith for reasons that then seemed to me sufficient, indeed compelling, but which, I must admit in retrospect, do credit to neither my character nor my intelligence. I had, however, prudently bolstered my defection with a number of specious arguments that served to rationalize it to my own satisfaction. I had also taken the precaution of never reading, or otherwise coming into contact with, anything that might challenge my atheistic worldview. If you want to stay an atheist, you can't be too careful! But, despite my best endeavours, I had encountered, through a combination of reading, music, life experience, and inward reflection, good grounds for calling my atheistic creed into question. The absence of a positive ground for atheism constitutes a negative ground for theism. What I still lacked were a) positive grounds for believing in Christianity, and b) grounds, whether positive or negative, for preferring one particular version of Christianity to any others.

However, before I could be motivated to look for these grounds in the right places, I had to undergo a final disillusionment with the wrong ones. I had already found much of what passed for secular philosophy a repulsively dry business. Some of it was, or seemed to me, the sort of thing a particularly arid kind of intellectual, one addicted to sterile debate for its own sake rather than as a means of discovering the truth, did for amusement. Rightly or wrongly, I thought such tedious logic-chopping of no more significance than an elaborate puzzle – a chess problem, say, or a cryptic crossword – and a lot less enjoyable. The idea of philosophy as the intellectually adventurous activity practised by Plato and Aristotle, or as the love of wisdom, which after all is what philosophy etymologically means, had given way, in some quarters, to the narrow and suffocating view that the role of philosophy was merely to clarify linguistic confusions (whether verbal, syntactical or grammatical) and establish the boundaries of the physical and social sciences. Like most people who are moved to study philosophy by curiosity about the basic human questions – such as 'What am I?' and 'How ought I to live?' – I had very little interest in such abstruse inquiries.

Nevertheless, I kept my loyalty to Russell and Sartre. True, they were poles apart philosophically, but politically they had much in common and their lives had certain similarities in terms of public political commitments, literary activities (both had been awarded the Nobel Prize, though Sartre had refused it), and an unwavering commitment to atheism. From a purely literary point of view, both were great writers, and I owed them too much and had been influenced by them too strongly, to turn my back on them now. From Russell, I had learned the importance of reasoning accurately, of drawing inferences carefully, of avoiding logical fallacies, and of basing beliefs on evidence and holding them just as firmly or as tentatively as the evidence warranted; from Sartre, I had learned the significance of freedom and autonomy, of the responsibility that comes with such freedom, of authenticity in one's choices and commitments, and of the danger of 'bad faith'. These were valuable lessons, and simply to reject writers from whom one had learned them because of a difference of view over religion, however profound that difference might be, would be an act of black ingratitude.

But my loyalty to both Russell and Sartre was now much qualified. It was severely jolted when I read their respective biographies and became acquainted, for the first time, with some of the details of their lives. First, both of them had left a trail of human havoc in their wake: wrecked personal relationships, broken friendships, ruined marriages and, in Russell's case, damaged children. Second, neither was able consistently to practise what he preached. For example, both believed in free love, which conveniently allowed them to satisfy their own inordinate sexual appetites. But both became jealous when their partners availed themselves of the same rights. Finally, both, by acting strictly in accordance with their published philosophical views, had advocated or condoned courses of action that were unequivocally evil. Russell had recommended a preëmptive nuclear strike by the United States on the Soviet Union, holding that the massive death and destruction that would inevitably result were a price worth paying for preventing the spread of nuclear weapons. Sartre defended the brutal Soviet repression of the 1956 uprising in Hungary and, much later, supported the Baader-Meinhof gang, perpetrators of a number of terrorist attacks. By their fruits ye shall know them. It seemed to me that philosophical beliefs that led logically to such obviously questionable commitments must be profoundly mistaken. It would, of course, be idle to deny that many Christians have, and have had, equally questionable commitments. The difference is that, in their case, those commitments did not follow logically from their Christian beliefs. There is no deductive process by which you can derive, from the proposition that you should love your neighbour and pray for your enemies, the conclusion that murder is justified. Therefore, when Christians committed atrocities, they did so in violation of their beliefs, not in accordance with them.

So, having found little satisfaction in secular philosophy, I was faced with the problem of where to look next for the answers to the moral and metaphysical questions that still concerned me. And I turned to something I had rejected over twenty years earlier. I turned to theology. But I soon found myself like a fell walker with no map and no compass, alone in the middle of a featureless terrain. Theology was a large and bewildering territory, of which I knew nothing. I knew of some Protestant and some Catholic theologians, but I had far less knowledge of the differences between them than I thought I had, and no idea where my reading ought to start. For some time, I read widely and indiscriminately. I read the Protestant theologians Karl Barth, Rudolf Bultmann, Paul Tillich, Dietrich Bonhoeffer and Wolfhart Pannenberg. I read the Catholic theologians Karl Rahner, Leonardo Boff, Leslie Dewart and John S. Dunne. I read the atheologians Don Cupitt and Lloyd Geering, and I read Ronald Gregor Smith, Ian Ramsey, David Jenkins and John Macquarrie. I read thinkers who defended Catholic orthodoxy and thinkers who attacked it. I read thinkers who claimed that the only religious realities were religious language and forms of worship, and thinkers who claimed that God was the ultimate reality. I read thinkers who claimed that God was immanent in history (whatever that meant) and thinkers who claimed that He transcended all human categories. I understood about half of what I read. I had a vague inkling of what some of the rest might mean. There was a substantial residuum that meant nothing at all that I could discover. After a couple of years of flailing about in the dark in this way, I was more confused than ever. I had discovered that I had never known what I ought to believe. Now I didn't even know what I *did* believe.

Clearly, I had to adopt a more methodical approach. For the moment, in relation to theology, I was like a man who opens a novel on the last page and then complains that he can't make head or tail of it. If I wanted to understand anything about theology, I should have to begin at the beginning. Many years earlier, a friend had lent me a copy of C. S. Lewis's *The Screwtape Letters*. I had returned it unread. I was then at the start of my existentialist phase. I read Camus and Sartre. What did I need with C. S. Lewis? An arrogant, bumptious and ignorant sixteen-year-old, I considered this brilliant Oxford scholar beneath my notice.

Not anymore. I bought a copy of *Mere Christianity*, the broadcast talks Lewis had given on the BBC during the war. I found, set out in crystalline prose, not only an argument in favour of Christianity to which I could think of no credible answer, but also convincing refutations of all the counter-arguments I had been trotting out by rote for the previous twenty-odd years. I found not only that my ideas were unoriginal, but also that they were untrue. I found that my view of the universe was riddled with contradictions, some of which I had become dimly aware of, while others were here revealed to me for the first time. I found that 'facts' I had taken for granted were not facts at all. I found my improvised *Weltanschauung*, assembled out of ill-assorted bits of other people's philosophy, first dismantled, and then utterly annihilated. Not even agnosticism was left as a possible 'fall back' position. Could I really claim, in the face of the existence of natural law, that it was impossible to know whether or not God existed? Even if I claimed that I didn't know whether He existed or not, could I make that claim on behalf of the entire human race, some of whom – including many notable for their veracity – claimed to have had religious experiences? Could I say that the mystical experiences of St John of the Cross, St Teresa of Ávila or Dame Julian of Norwich, were invalid, that they were evidentially worthless? It seemed to me that, when people whose word one has no reason to doubt, make claims, those claims should be heard seriously and examined on their merits, not dismissed in accordance with a dogmatic presumption in favour of materialism. And when the people concerned are not merely people whose word one has no reason to doubt, but people whose word one has very good reasons to credit, then to dismiss their claims out of hand seems worse than mistaken: it seems foolish and perverse.

But I wasn't ready to throw in the towel just yet. I realized intellectually that, for me, atheism was no longer tenable, and that even agnosticism was not available as a protection against a belief I was still very reluctant to accept. But habits of thought and belief become ingrained over time. I simply could not accept that most of what I had thought for the past thirty years about the most important things was wrong – and not only wrong, but diametrically opposed to the truth; that I had been mistaken about nearly everything that mattered; or that I had based my supposedly rational beliefs on the intellectual equivalent of a foundation of sand. It was too much to take in. My mind rebelled violently against what seemed an ineluctable conclusion. Later, I realized, from my reading and from this personal experience, that the human mind is quite capable, when it suits its purposes to do so, of simultaneously entertaining two or more contradictory opinions. In my case, I now had sufficient grounds for accepting the truth claims of Christianity. But I still would not do it. I wanted more evidence, more certainty, before I would abandon the views I had held for thirty years, even though they now seemed to me to have been thoroughly discredited. In Newman's language, my will stubbornly refused to assent to what my intellect understood to be the case.

At least, I now knew where to look to find the evidence I required. For almost thirty years, I had read practically nothing but materialist philosophy and literature. Wherever possible, I had avoided religious writers, except a few who, as it were, had crossed my path by chance. Now, belatedly, tentatively at first, but then enthusiastically, I began to explore the literature of Christian apologetics. I was amazed at how extensive and varied it was. In a supposedly secular age, an immense quantity of apologetic literature had been generated, some by lay writers, often of great distinction, some by professional philosophers and theologians. I started by reading everything of Lewis that I could find. His *The Problem of Pain* effectively disposed of any lingering suspicion on my part that the atheistic argument from innocent suffering was fatal to Christianity. *The Screwtape Letters* proved to be a witty and sardonic look at the evasive strategies the mind employs in order to get out of disagreeable duties, or avoid having to accept unpalatable beliefs for which it has found compelling evidence. *The Four Loves* was an exegesis of the nature of the different varieties of love as subtle, as beautifully written, and as exquisitely reasoned, as anything I had ever read.

It has always been my experience that, in reading as in life, one thing leads to another. I have already mentioned how my interest in writers from the American South eventually led me to the works of Flannery O'Connor. In the same way, my reading of Lewis led me to the apologetic works of two other notable writers: his friend Dorothy L. Sayers, and his mentor G. K. Chesterton. In both, I found the same combination of robust good humour and rationality that I had found in Lewis. And I was struck by a note in their writings that I had not encountered in the essays of Russell, or Sartre, or Ayer, or any of the atheistic, materialist philosophers who claimed to represent pure reason against the blind forces of irrationality, prejudice and superstition. At first, I wasn't sure what this note was. But then, suddenly, it came to me. It was the note of *health*, of *sanity*. It was the note of harmony between intellect and conscience, mind and morals, truth and goodness. A view that saw the existence of the universe as accidental, the product of blind chance, but nevertheless insisted that human life had intrinsic value, that art had meaning, that philosophy (or anything else) mattered, was incoherent. It was trying to have it both ways: to say both that something mattered and that (ultimately) nothing mattered; that life had a purpose, and that life ended in death and oblivion; that art had meaning, and that all the greatest art was delusional or meaningless. In order to entertain such beliefs, one had to become a split personality: one had to divide one's mind into hermetically sealed compartments, one containing truth, the other, values. One could not admit even the merest possibility of any connexion between them. For Lewis, Sayers and Chesterton, on the other hand, truth and goodness were intimately – in fact, inextricably – connected. They were related in having a common source, a Creator who was the fount and origin of all truth, wisdom, goodness and beauty. It was this integrity, this wholeness, this relatedness of all parts to the whole that gave their thought its sense of harmony, coherence and sanity. And it was precisely these qualities that I could not find anywhere in the atheistic literature and philosophy that I had studied exclusively for so long. I had, I finally realized, rejected atheism, not from any sense of emotional or psychological need that atheism was unable to satisfy, but because it did not satisfy my reason. A system of beliefs that required its adherents to separate and compartmentalize their views about truth and value, rather than integrating them by insisting that the latter be grounded in the former, was irrational. It was unwilling to face the logical consequences of its view of truth.

So far, so good. I had arrived at the point where both my will and my intellect were ready to assent to Christianity. But to what sort of Christianity? Catholicism? Anglicanism? One of the evangelical Protestant churches? If so, which one? The Baptist? The Methodist? The Presbyterian? Did it matter? Was it even necessary to declare one's allegiance, to go beyond the confession that one was a Christian? But then I came back to the question that had started all the trouble: into which Church should I be baptized? The necessity of baptism was clear, not only from the words of Christ, but also from his example. Very well, then. But one could not just be baptized, as Christ was: one had to be baptized into a particular church to which one's allegiance would thereafter be pledged. But which one?

The Claims of the
Catholic Church

In fairness, I had to examine the claims of both Catholicism and Protestantism (at least, in general – I could, if necessary, proceed later to a scrutiny of the claims of rival denominations) to teach the truth. I decided to start with the Catholic Church, first, because the theological literature and historiography were much vaster in relation to Catholicism than in relation to any of the other varieties of Christianity; and, second, because my reading at the time was tending in that direction anyway. It is true that C. S. Lewis and Dorothy L. Sayers were Anglicans, but there was little in their published writings on religion with which a Catholic would take issue, and much that would seem strange to the majority of modern Anglicans. The same could be said of Charles Williams and T. S. Eliot.

It was during this period that I first became acquainted with three books that strongly influenced my subsequent thinking: Newman's *Apologia Pro Vita Sua* and Ronald Knox's *A Spiritual Aeneid* and *The Belief of Catholics*. The first two of these were spiritual autobiographies and displayed striking similarities. Each told, in exquisite prose, how a distinguished Anglican clergyman and academic had converted to Catholicism after becoming convinced, on the historical evidence, that the Catholic Church alone had a valid claim to

authority in matters of Christian doctrine. The third book –
The Belief of Catholics – was an admirably clear and succinct
account of what Catholics believe and why. It was written
before the Second Vatican Council and is therefore dated in
some minor respects, but, in all essentials, it remains probably
the best short exposition of Catholic belief to have been
written in English. It is sad that Knox, one of the most learned,
literate, elegant, and accomplished prose writers of his day, is
now so little read.

I had long known that the Catholic Church made a number
of startling claims. Crucially, it claimed

- to be the one, true, holy, catholic and apostolic
  Church founded by Jesus Christ himself;
- that the Catholic Church, and only the Catholic
  Church, had authority from Christ to absolve sins,
  pronounce doctrinal judgments, and decide on
  matters of ecclesiastical discipline, in his name;
- that its bishops were the lineal descendants of the
  Apostles by Apostolic Succession; and
- that it was preserved by the promises of Christ from
  teaching error in matters of faith and morals.

What I had not examined in any detail before was the grounds
on which those claims were made. To my surprise, I learned
from Newman and Knox that the grounds were not, as I had
supposed, Church tradition, but Scripture. Moreover, Church
tradition and Scripture were not separate entities, as I had also
supposed, but intertwined. The Scriptural canon itself was a
matter of Church tradition. It was the early Church that had

decided which of the gospels and other texts were canonical and which were not. Even the office of bishops (bishop = *episcopos* = overseer), which I had ignorantly thought to be a later invention, proved to be a feature of the Church from the earliest times, and one amply evidenced by the Acts of the Apostles and by the Pauline epistles.

This, of course, raised a question: if the Church founded by Christ was one (that is, if, in the technical language of theology, unity was a *note* of the Church), then how could the schism of the Protestant Reformation be justified? To put it another way, if the Church had been right in what it taught for a millennium and a half, as all Western Christians apparently believed, then how and why did it suddenly become wrong? The Protestant reformers alleged that the Church had become rotten and corrupt, and that therefore it could no longer be considered the Church of Christ. But this is a *non sequitur*. The promises of Christ were as follows—

> 'Thou art Peter and on this Rock I will build my Church…and the gates of hell will not prevail against it…. I will give you the keys of the kingdom. Whatsoever you bind on earth shall be considered bound in heaven and whatsoever you loose on earth shall be considered loosed in heaven…. Whose sins you forgive, they are forgiven; whose sins you retain, they are retained…. For behold I am with you even to the end of time.'

Throughout the history of the Church, these promises have been understood to mean that the Church would not be suffered to teach error. They do not mean that the Church will always be led by wise, good, or courageous men. They do not mean that every act of every Church representative or leader will be a good act, in any sense of the term. They do not mean that a faithful Catholic is required to defend or condone – much less to approve – everything that has been done in the Church's name, from the sale of indulgences to the crimes of the Inquisition. They do not mean that Church leaders may speak with authority on subjects outside their remit. They mean quite simply what they say: and it follows that the Church will not be suffered to teach error in those matters that fall within its purview; and that therefore entire reliance may be placed on what the Church teaches as official doctrine in matters of faith and morals.

It seemed to me that, if the claims of the Catholic Church were valid from the first, then they remained valid today. Either they were right from the first, or they were wrong – also from the first. It did not seem to me plausible to suppose that they could have been right for a millennium and a half, and then suddenly have become wrong.

So the question was: were the Church's claims valid from the first or not? It was to this question that I now turned.

I had not confined my reading to the Catholic theologians and philosophers. I had also continued to read the major Protestant writers and thinkers of the twentieth century. I found in their works a strange and confusing medley of ideas. To cite a few examples: I encountered, in the writings of the Anglican (formerly Presbyterian) theologian and sometime Lady Margaret Professor of Divinity at Oxford, John Macquarrie, an existentialist approach based on the philosophy of Heidegger and the theology of Rudolf Bultmann. This approach emphasized the primacy, for the believing subject, of encounter with God's Word in the *kerygma* (the preaching or proclamation of the Word from the pulpit). Macquarrie appeared to accept the need for 'demythologizing' the New Testament in order to bring it into harmony with modern knowledge. Thus the text was to be purged of any miraculous and supernatural elements – of anything, in short, that a modern, scientistic worldview had difficulty in accommodating. Similarly, the charismatic Methodist preacher and theologian, Leslie Weatherhead – whom my mother had often heard preach at the City Temple Church in London in the 1940s – rejected such central and credal Christian doctrines as the Atonement, the Trinity, the Virgin Birth, and the Resurrection, and regarded St Paul as a neurotic, though Weatherhead's approach, unlike Macquarrie's, was grounded not in existentialism, but in a confused mixture of Freudian psychology, spiritualism, and Eastern religion (he apparently believed in reincarnation). In the works of Albert Schweitzer, too, particularly in his *The Quest for the Historical Jesus*, I found a rejection of much that traditional Christianity taught and believed, including, it seemed, the divinity of Christ. In Don Cupitt and Lloyd Geering, I found a 'non-realist' theology (more properly, an atheology) supposedly grounded in the philosophy of Wittgenstein: according to these thinkers, the only religious realities are religious language and forms of worship (but worship of what exactly, I wanted to ask).

Much modern theology, Catholic as well as Protestant, was couched in terms so obscure that it was far from clear to me what the author meant. But three things were abundantly clear. First, if Christians themselves were not united in what they taught and believed, they had very little chance of convincing others. Second, this pick-and-mix approach, which has been aptly described as 'cafeteria Christianity', treats the Christian faith not as objective truth, but as a matter of personal taste. Everyone is free to take what he likes and leave the rest. This is not compatible with either the Gospels or the apostolic teaching of the early Church. And third, the beliefs of at least some modern Protestant thinkers were not only considerably at variance with each other, or with what the Church has taught historically: they were also very far from what the original Protestant reformers had taught. There is little doubt that Luther, Calvin, and Zwingli would have been horrified by Schweitzer and Bultmann, or that Wesley would have disowned Weatherhead. Nor can these differences be attributed to doctrinal developments. What we are dealing with in Bultmann and Macquarrie, Schweitzer and Weatherhead, Cupitt and Geering, is not a logical development of Christian doctrine, but a straightforward repudiation of it.

Despite the difference between what the original Protestant reformers taught and wanted, and what had subsequently become of the movement they initiated, it seemed to me that the seeds of the later revolts and schisms were present in the earlier. Luther aimed at doing away with all mediæval accretions and corruptions and returning to a purer, more Biblical and patristic Christianity. But who, in that case, was to decide what was 'pure', 'Biblical' and 'patristic' and what was a corruption? Where was the locus of authority? Who could adjudicate in cases of disagreement? Who had the right to interpret Scripture and tradition authoritatively? Because Protestantism never had credible answers to these questions; because in effect it made the individual sovereign and his judgment final; because it exalted the freedom and autonomy of the individual believer above the authority of the Church, future schisms were, from the first, inevitable. Protestants – whether they were early reformers like Luther and Calvin, or modern ones like Macquarrie and Weatherhead – neither acknowledged, nor could appeal to, any authority higher than their private judgment.

These reflections did not enable me to decide whether or not the claims of the Roman Catholic Church were valid, but they did prove to my satisfaction that the claims of any form of Protestantism to be the custodian of Christian truth could safely be rejected with a good logical conscience. It was not credible either that the Church should have been right in its doctrinal teaching for a millennium and a half and then suddenly have gone astray, or that any of the other contending bodies had a better claim than the Catholic Church to speak with authority on questions relating to the doctrine of the Christian Faith. But the question remained: what exactly was the Catholic Church? Was it co-extensive with the Church of Rome? In other words, were the claims of the Roman Catholic Church true? Or did the Catholic Church comprise also other churches not in communion with Rome? Granted that it was incredible that God should have intervened in human history in such an extraordinary way as the Incarnation and left no means of preserving his revelation intact for posterity, was that means the Roman Catholic Church?

Interlude

interlude

A Film and Two Books

At some point when I was mulling over the great religious questions, I saw Claude Goretta's remarkable film, *La Dentellière* (1977, translated *The Lacemaker*), based on a Prix Goncourt-winning 1974 novel by Pascal Lainé and starring the luminous French actress, Isabelle Huppert. The film tells the story of a love affair between Béatrice, a shy young beautician (Isabelle Huppert), and François, a university student (Yves Beneyton). At first, François is attracted to the young girl, partly by her guileless innocence. Their affair begins when they are both on vacation. François is Béatrice's first lover but it seems unlikely that he is without previous experience. After the vacation, she moves into his flat in Paris. She cooks and cleans for him after finishing work at the beauty parlour so that he can pursue his studies. They seem happy together. But gradually François becomes bored with her, irritated by her self-effacing ways, lack of conversation, and what he sees as her inability to compete with his intellectual friends. He suggests disingenuously that it will be better for both of them to break up, and returns her to her mother's apartment. Béatrice, typically, does not oppose François' proposal, but is deeply distressed. Back at her mother's flat, she is unable to eat and grows steadily weaker until, one day, she collapses in the street. She is taken to a sanatorium where François, belatedly stricken with guilt for his selfish and callous behaviour, visits her. Béatrice, who has clearly suffered a nervous breakdown, responds mechanically to his questions. In an autumnal scene, they sit together in a park. François asks her what she has been doing since they broke up and Béatrice tells him that she has had other lovers and describes a trip to Greece with one of them. François seems relieved, evidently feeling that her admission exonerates him from responsibility for her past pain, her present misery, and her uncertain future. As he leaves, Béatrice gazes after him, and her expression subtly changes to a haunting look of infinite hurt and reproach. In the next shot, the camera tracks in on a room where Béatrice sits alone in a corner, knitting in front of a gaudy poster of Mykonos. Her trip to Greece was an invention, both a deception and a farewell gift for François allowing him to return to his self-serving existence with a clear conscience. As the truth dawns, she turns to the camera with a lost and tragic expression that Goretta then freezes. The closing titles appear. He had never really seen her because he had never looked at her. In a painting by one of the Old Masters, she would have been one of the anonymous working women – a seamstress, perhaps, or a water girl. Or perhaps…a lacemaker. Thus only at the very end of the film does the significance of the title become clear.

The Lacemaker is an unforgettable film of great subtlety, poignancy and depth. Essentially, it tells the story of the sort of life that, all too often, is simply overlooked. Béatrice, a simple, innocent girl, will never be what the world sees as a success. Her ambitions do not go beyond fulfilling a few ordinary, humble and very human needs: finding someone to love and be loved by, raising a family, enjoying simple pleasures, and enduring whatever sorrows she must. But, for all the intellectual differences between them, she is infinitely deeper than François; infinitely more capable than he of love, loyalty, honesty, courage and commitment. He, in contrast, is shallow, egocentric, narcissistic; incapable of emotional depth, of truly loving another person, of taking responsibility for the consequences of his acts, or of telling or facing up to the truth. He can only prattle about the moral life with his equally superficial friends. He cannot live it.

About the time I first saw *The Lacemaker*, I read two fine novels by the inexplicably neglected English writer, F. M. Mayor – *The Rector's Daughter* and *The Third Miss Symons*. Both concerned middle-aged spinsters, but there the resemblance ended. In the first, Mary Jocelyn, the eponymous rector's daughter, is a woman in her thirties who has lived a contented life of quiet utility to others until a new curate arrives in the village. She falls in love with him and believes, not entirely without reason, that he loves her. But he marries someone else. Mary has to endure not only the shock, shame and pain of rejection, but also the public spectacle and private knowledge of her supposed suitor's happy marriage. Despite her desolating sense of loss and loneliness, she resumes her life of humble service and never shows outwardly the pain she feels, which no one even guesses until after her death.

In the second, Henrietta Symons is, on the face of it, an unsympathetic protagonist. She is ill-tempered, narrow and opinionated. But she, too, has known pain. She, like Mary, has an inner life which is concealed from the world – a life of hidden disappointment and suffering, ignored by those around her. She is lonely and embittered, a spinster who has missed her chance of marriage. Her diffident and awkward temperament, her lack of what today would be called 'social skills', cause her to be regarded by most other people as difficult, unlovable, and finally not worth bothering with. Although she longs to be needed, to love, and to be loved, she cannot change what she is. She cannot do any of the things she desperately wants to do except by becoming a different person, an obvious impossibility. She is condemned, by a temperament she cannot help having, to a useless life: a life of boredom, loneliness, frustration, unwanted love and thwarted hopes. And yet, *The Third Miss Symons* ends, after Henrietta's death, on a note of hope, when her surviving younger sister, the only person who had ever felt any kind of sympathy for her, experiences an epiphany that leaves her convinced that Henrietta has at last found the happiness she sought.

The Lacemaker, The Rector's Daughter, and *The Third Miss Symons* are alike in being concerned with forgotten lives – the sort of lives that ordinarily pass unnoticed. The qualities that Béatrice, Mary and Henrietta have to offer – for example, the silent courage with which they bear their crosses – are not valued in a world that worships success, and measures success solely in terms of wealth, possessions, status, and power. François is initially attracted to Béatrice – but when the physical attraction wanes and boredom supervenes, he discards her without compunction. True, he comes, eventually, to feel remorse for his actions. But the first selfish action is the hardest. One's conscience when young, before it has had a chance to become hardened, is tender, and its voice is too strong to be altogether silenced. But the next betrayal will be easier. And the one after that, and so on, until the voice of conscience, inured to such conduct, no longer even raises a protest. Mary, quiet and reserved, makes little impression on others. Even her poetry, once admired, is later cruelly and casually dismissed as 'the usual Anglican spinster warbling'. Her virtues – loyalty, self-denial, her capacity for love, her silent endurance of pain – are not even remarked. And, while Henrietta is a less attractive character than Béatrice or Mary, she is, in some ways, the most to be pitied, since her life lacks even the bleak consolations of self-sacrifice that theirs can claim.

So what follows? To an atheist, such lives can only be a tragic or absurd waste. They possess no intrinsic value whatsoever. For Sartre, each human individual makes himself what he is through the decisions he takes and the consciously willed acts he performs in the actual course of living. The majority of human beings perform no such acts and can only be considered as nonentities. Béatrice, Mary and Henrietta would unquestionably fall into this category. Russell, throughout his voluminous output, treats intelligence not as a gift, like a beautiful singing voice, but as a virtue. Sometimes he seems almost to regard it as the supreme virtue, as when he remarks caustically, evidently seeing it as a damning criticism, that he can find no word in praise of intelligence in any of the Gospels. And, when he speaks of those who, in his judgment, lack intelligence, he invariably alternates between pity tinged with condescension, and contempt. By Russell's standards, none of these women would be regarded as highly intelligent and none, therefore, would be seen as highly valuable. For Nietzsche, they would belong to the 'bungled and botched' –

the great mass of humanity who, lacking the ruthlessness of the *Übermensch*, are fit only to be slaves. For Marx, they would be atomized members of the hated *petite bourgeoisie*, obstacles to the revolution, and enemies of the proletariat. To Freud, they would merely be casebook studies in neurosis, and nothing more. And note that these views are strictly entailed by the philosophy professed by the thinkers to whom they are severally attributed.

Yet what is the Christian view? For the Christian, each human being is fashioned in the *imago Dei*. Each human being is loved by God and, because God loves each of us, we are commanded to love each other. Nor is this love merely a sentiment. According to the Christian view, that each human being is fashioned in God's image (i.e. is endowed with a rational soul) is a fact. That God loves each of us is a fact. That we should love God as the source and sustainer of our lives and of everything that is good, is a fact. And, if these are facts, then it is also a fact that we should love each other, as Christ commanded; and that means treating each other with respect, with care, and with due regard for each other's needs, feelings, wants, and so on. It follows that lives such as those we have been considering are not just of value, but of inexpressible value. They are valued by God – so much so that, for such as these, he took on human form and died on a Cross. That is the Christian view.

So we have two worldviews: according to the first, the lives of Béatrice, Mary and Henrietta are worthless because of their lack of committed actions, or intelligence, or ruthlessness, or psychological health (as the case may be): according to the second, they are of infinite value because they are loved by

God. There may be arguments as to which of these views is more probably true. There can surely be no doubt as to which is more conducive to moral goodness or to sanity. Logically, anyone who holds the first view to be true should see no difference between the death of a person such as Béatrice, Mary or Henrietta and that of a cockroach. Logically, anyone who holds the second view must see their death as an occasion for mourning their passing, giving thanks for their lives, and praying for their souls. Which of these is the saner, healthier, more humane attitude? Put it another way: which of these two worldviews would you want your children to adopt?

Encountering Jesus

I have said something about the differences between Catholicism and Protestantism, and the reasons why I was drawn to the former and rejected the latter. But I have not so far said anything about what all Christians have in common: namely, a belief (in some sense) in Jesus of Nazareth.

For many people today, the name of Jesus Christ is simply a convenient ejaculation to express surprise, annoyance, exasperation, alarm, wonder, or whatever other emotion is currently agitating their mind. They know, or imagine they know, the outlines of the Christian story and the basics of the Christian faith. In fact, the standard of religious knowledge and religious education in Britain today is woeful; and very few people younger than fifty have an understanding of religion in general, or Christianity in particular, which goes beyond the rudimentary.

So who exactly was Jesus? Pope Benedict XVI's magisterial three-volume *Jesus of Nazareth* poses the question, what does Jesus offer? What is unique and distinctive about Jesus? What does he offer us that cannot be got from anyone else? And the answer is: God. From the Annunciation to the Ascension, the gospel narrative makes it consistently clear that Jesus is not a prophet like Elijah or John the Baptist, nor a teacher like Socrates or Confucius, nor a sage like the Buddha or

Zoroaster. He is unique: the Son of God, both fully human and fully divine, the second person of the Trinity, and co-equal with God the Father. Now, one can accept that claim or reject it. But what one cannot reasonably do is to accept some radically diluted version of the gospel claim (for example, that Jesus was a great moral teacher but was not divine) and present that as a new form of Christianity, deserving of belief and superior in important respects to Christian orthodoxy.

What did Jesus teach? The first thing to say is that his teaching is much richer and more complex than the popular version of it suggests. The key themes are as follows—

REPENT OF YOUR SINS

This obviously links with the Catholic sacrament of penance. Repentance has three components: confession, contrition, and a firm purpose of amendment. Sins must be owned up to, the sinner must be genuinely sorry for the wrong s/he has done, and must have a firm intention not to repeat the offence. Jesus calls each of us to repair what is broken, to make good what is wanting. This is unfashionable in an age that regards feelings of guilt and remorse not as morally appropriate responses to the knowledge that one has done something wrong, but as symptoms of neurosis, and that sees humility (an obvious prerequisite to repentance) as a sign of either weakness or hypocrisy.

BELIEVE AND BE BAPTIZED

Jesus lays great emphasis on the importance of belief. Again and again he insists upon this to his followers.

Wrestling With the Angel

'Believe and be baptized.' 'Blessed are they who have not seen and yet have believed.' 'He that believeth in me, though he were dead, yet shall he live.' 'For this is the will of my Father, that every one that beholdeth the Son and believeth on him should have eternal life, and I will raise him up at the Last Day.' 'Believe in God, believe also in me.' Belief – an attitude of absolute, unqualified trust in God and in Jesus himself – is the necessary foundation for a rational faith. And the ceremony of baptism is the public profession of faith, the avowal of one's belief in Christ and intention to follow him.

FORGIVE THOSE WHO HAVE WRONGED YOU

Jesus combines exhortations to forgive others for any wrongs they may have done to oneself with stern warnings of what awaits those who reject his teaching. The Lord's Prayer contains the petition, 'Forgive us our trespasses as we forgive those who trespass against us.' In other words, we can expect forgiveness only if we grant forgiveness. If we do not, we can expect justice untempered by mercy. We can expect, in other words, to be judged with the same severity that we have shown to others. And there is no limit to the number of times we must grant forgiveness: not seven times, but seventy times seven, we are told – which is to say, we must grant forgiveness whenever it is sought. We are forbidden ever to harbour grudges or resentment.

PRAY FOR YOUR ENEMIES

It is generally true that, as C. S. Lewis said, Christian

morality is just morality *tout court*. But, if there is a revolutionary element in Christian moral teaching, this is it. Certainly the notion that one should pray for one's enemies, rather than for their destruction, was – and is – alien to the Jewish tradition; and it seems equally so to Islam, which, like Judaism, accepts the *lex talionis*: 'an eye for an eye…'. For Jesus, however, we must sincerely desire our enemies' good, and pray for it. And this links with his teaching on forgiveness. We are forbidden, on pain of the severest penalties, to wish ill to anyone. Mercy – of which we all stand in the direst need, for we are all sinners – is reserved to the merciful.

LOVE GOD AND LOVE YOUR NEIGHBOUR

These, Jesus tells us, are the commandments under which all the others are comprehended: 'Thou shalt love the Lord thy God with thy whole heart, and with thy whole soul, and with all thy strength, and with all thy mind: and thy neighbour as thyself.' If you truly love your neighbour, you will not covet anything that is his, or bear false witness against him. If you truly love God, you will keep his commandments – not from fear of the consequences of transgression, but from disinterested love of God.

KEEP THE COMMANDMENTS

It is sometimes alleged that Jesus preached a religion of love, not law, and that this distinguishes Christianity from both Judaism and Islam, which are essentially legalistic faiths. At best, this is a half-truth. Jesus tells his disciples that he has come to fulfil the law, not to abolish it. Matthew 5: 17–20 reads as follows: 'Think not that I came to destroy the law or the prophets: I came not to destroy, but to fulfil. For verily I say unto you, Till heaven and earth pass away, one jot or one tittle shall in no wise pass away from the law, till all things be accomplished. Whosoever therefore shall break one of these least commandments, and shall teach men so, shall be called least in the kingdom of heaven: but whosoever shall do and teach them, he shall be called great in the kingdom of heaven. For I say unto you, that except your righteousness shall exceed the righteousness of the scribes and Pharisees, ye shall in no wise enter into the kingdom of heaven.'

THE KINGDOM OF HEAVEN IS AT HAND

Jesus continually insists that the kingdom of heaven is at hand, but also that the kingdom of heaven is not of this world. This, like the call to repentance, is a difficult teaching for many today. It is a warning against any attempt to reduce the gospel to social work, as some believe movements such as the worker priests in France and liberation theology in Latin America tried to do. The kingdom of heaven is the realm of justice, mercy, charity and truth. It is something to which we look for a final reckoning and a perfectly just judgment, one which will right the wrongs and correct the injustices done in this world. But it is not attainable in this world, or by any merely human efforts, unassisted by grace.

RECEIVE THE SACRAMENTS

I have already mentioned the link between Jesus' call to repentance and the sacrament of penance (or reconciliation). But, quite clearly, there is also a link between the Eucharistic discourse in Chapter Six of St John's Gospel and the practice of receiving holy communion – the practice that lies at the heart of the Catholic Mass. 'He that eateth my flesh, and drinketh my blood, hath everlasting life: and I will raise him up in the last day,' says Jesus. And 'I tell you the truth, unless you eat the flesh of the Son of Man and drink his blood, you have no life in you.' There can be no clearer injunction to take the sacraments than this. It is not an optional extra, but a belief that is essential to Christianity.

PREACH THE GOSPEL

Jesus makes clear that the gospel is for all men: it is not an esoteric doctrine reserved for a few *illuminati*. Nor is it to be confined to the Jews. Implicit in Jesus' command, 'Go ye into all the world and preach the gospel' is an attitude of total openness towards the world, to Jew and Gentile alike. This openness, this refusal to think in the narrow, exclusivist terms of in-group/out-group psychology, is one of the marks that distinguishes Christianity from other religions. Historically, it has often brought Christianity into conflict with other faiths because the command to preach the gospel also implies a conscious attempt to proselytize. This may be problematic, but it is a duty that must not be shirked.

CULTIVATE THE VIRTUES

Jesus lays equal stress on virtuous *dispositions* (love God, love your neighbour) and virtuous *behaviour* (pray for your enemies, do good to others), with a clear implication that the latter follows from the former. Without virtuous dispositions, there can be no virtuous intentions, and without virtuous intentions, there can be no virtuous behaviour. But the Christian view of the virtues is today so unfamiliar, so deeply and thoroughly counter-cultural, that it is worth spending a little time considering it.

The theological virtues: faith, hope and charity. Charity in the Christian sense (i.e. love, *agape*) is still widely recognized today as a virtue. But faith is often equated with superstition or blind credulity, and hope with foolish optimism. The notion of faith as a rational attitude of trust in that which has proved itself worthy of trust, or of eschatological hope as the opposite of despair, is not properly understood. A better understanding of the theological virtues would confirm their indispensability to a moral life that is not only rational but also rich and imaginative.

The cardinal virtues: prudence, justice, temperance, fortitude. The cardinal virtues, too, are not always rightly understood. Prudence is thought to mean caution. In fact, it means rather what we should call wisdom: the faculty of right judgment. Temperance is regarded as abstinence from alcohol. In fact, it has a much wider meaning, encompassing what we would probably call self-restraint or self-control. Justice does not refer to a purely legal concept, but rather to what we would probably call fairness or equity. Only fortitude or courage bears precisely the same meaning today as it would have had for both classical or mediæval scholars.

The evangelical virtues: poverty, chastity, humility and obedience. It is with the evangelical virtues that the disparity between Christian and modern, secular thinking becomes acute. In a world in which the pursuit of wealth is regarded as self-evidently good, and political decisions are dictated by economic considerations, voluntary poverty is seen as perverse and pointless. In a world in which even children are sexualized, chastity is seen as either synonymous with, or symptomatic of, frigidity. In a world in which assertiveness is promoted and psychologists encourage patients to cultivate self-esteem, humility is seen as either hypocritical (if feigned) or neurotic (if genuine). In a world in which all authority is suspect, obedience is seen as craven and subservient. The notion that these virtues are aspects of a rightly ordered relationship with God is not entertained, let alone understood.

Coming Home

M$_y$ position just before my conversion might be summarized as follows. I had arrived at the conclusion that Christianity was morally saner and healthier than any alternative, and at the further conclusion that it was true. I based this conclusion on the empirical fact that, whereas Christianity, in its Catholic form, was capable of harmonizing my moral intuitions with my cosmology, materialist philosophies were not. I had rejected Protestant forms of Christianity as incoherent. The only inevitable result of placing one's trust in private judgment was a chaos of competing, mutually inconsistent opinions, none of which could appeal to any higher authority for support, or demonstrate why its rivals should be rejected and its own claim to authority upheld.

The alternative to a *de facto* deification of private judgment is to accept some form of external authority in matters relating to faith and morals. The only locus of authority I could find whose claims seemed legitimate was the Catholic Church. Now, it must be admitted that the arguments for accepting the Church's authority are circular. The Church is our primary source of knowledge of Christ, since it predates the documents that compose the New Testament. But Christ is also the founder of the Church. Thus the Church guarantees Christ;

and Christ, as its founder, guarantees the Church. We find similar paradoxes elsewhere in our argument. For instance—

- A correctly formed conscience leads us to accept the teaching authority of the Church BUT the Church's authority is also answerable before the tribunal of the individual conscience.

- The Church decided in the first century what made up the canon of Scripture BUT the Church herself is subject to Scripture: she cannot, even in the twenty-first century, violate what Scripture decrees.

To some, the circularity of these arguments invalidates them, and nothing more need be said. But we have already seen that the arguments against the existence of God are *petitios*, quite as much as the arguments for His existence. When all is said and done, philosophy cannot settle for us the question of religious belief. Neither can science, for religious questions, by definition, lie outside the realm of what can be established by scientific methods of inquiry. Philosophically speaking, either belief or unbelief is a venture. The appeal of religion is not to the strict sequential reasoning of logical argument, nor to the empirical reasoning of the sciences, but to the general sense-making and truth-seeking capacities of the human mind. We strive as far as possible to harmonize all our philosophical beliefs, so that they are mutually consistent. The Catholic Faith enables us to harmonize metaphysical beliefs on the one hand, and our moral intuitions on the other, in a way achieved by no other belief system known to me.

It is not only intellectually – rationally – that Christianity makes sense. It also makes emotional and imaginative sense. Who would be so perverse as to believe, in his heart of hearts, that emotions such as love of God (love, that is, of the *summum bonum*), love of neighbour, kindness, compassion, empathy, mercy, forgiveness, mildness, generosity and peace, should not be cultivated? And what of feelings such as guilt, sorrow and remorse for sin, or joy, gladness and thankfulness at the news of redemption? Are not these humanly natural emotional responses? Who truly believes, when he examines the innermost convictions of his conscience, that these qualities, these emotions and reactions, are morally wrong or emotionally inapposite, or that their opposites should be preferred? Even the evangelical virtues, which, as noted above, are generally misunderstood, and are currently out of fashion – can anyone who truly *thinks* about them objectively and rationally, who makes the effort required to grasp what they mean, who sets aside the prejudices of the day and reflects upon the consequences of acting on these emotions and applying them in practice – can anyone who does all this honestly say that he would have done better to have acted otherwise?

Does one have to be a Christian in order to approve of Christian emotions? No: it is open to anyone to choose to cultivate such emotions – if he wants to. Christianity simply gives one a compelling reason to want to. What the intelligibility of Christian emotions shows is the deep consonance that exists between Christianity and our most profound moral intuitions. This consonance is unsurprising if Christianity is true. It would be very surprising indeed if Christianity were false.

The historicity of Christianity is also an important dimension since Christianity, to an extent unmatched by any other faith, focuses not on a putatively scriptural text but on a person. Those who reject the divinity of Jesus must decide for themselves what to make of this uniquely challenging and profoundly enigmatic figure. Lewis's trilemma illustrates the extreme difficulty of making sense of the historical figure of Jesus of Nazareth without accepting his claims about himself and his relation to God.

So: we believe in Christ because Christianity makes sense of the totality of our experience. Christianity makes sense of the totality of our experience because it harmonizes our cosmology and our historical knowledge with our moral intuitions. It harmonizes our cosmology with our moral intuitions because it regards the universe as the outcome not of random forces, but of the purposive activity of a mind: thus, order, purpose, pattern and design are built into the universe and our moral intuitions form part of such order, purpose, pattern and design, and themselves exhibit precisely those attributes. It harmonizes our historical knowledge of Jesus with our moral intuitions because it accepts Jesus' claims about himself and thus grants a unique authority to his moral teaching, which exhibits a deep consonance with the innermost voice of our conscience.

Now, throughout history, the body that has carefully preserved, developed, transmitted, and defended the Christian Faith in the Western world; that has deduced consequences and drawn inferences from the apostolic faith; that has defined doctrines and opposed heresies; that has combated the rising tide of secularism and atheism; that has insisted on the logical connexion between metaphysical dogma and moral precept; that has taken the gospel to the furthest ends of the earth; that has laboured among the poor, the oppressed and the sick; that has built not only churches, monasteries and convents, but also schools, colleges, clinics, hospitals and orphanages; that has sent priests and religious to work amid terrible dangers, in plague areas, leper colonies, war zones, and areas of crippling poverty; that, as a provider of aid to the Third World, is second only to the United Nations; that, with 1.3 billion members worldwide, is not only incomparably the largest organization the world has ever known but also the one that has enjoyed the longest continuous existence – that body is the Roman Catholic Church. No other body can claim as much. None even comes close.

Considerations such as these obliged me, by degrees, to be received into the Church of Rome as a believing Catholic. Chesterton says somewhere that the Church is much bigger on the inside than it looks from the outside. That has certainly been my experience. Since my reception, I have tried to explore the amazing patrimony of Catholic art, literature, liturgy, philosophy and theology. In twelve years, I have not even scratched the surface. It is the work of a lifetime – or, rather, of several lifetimes. In a sense, one never simply *is* a Catholic. One is in a constant state of *becoming*. And becoming a Catholic is an art, a process, a journey, a pilgrimage, a discipline, an education. It is all of these and much, much more. It is a gift, and an extraordinary enrichment of one's spiritual and intellectual life. It is necessary to insist on this because, to many outside the Church, it seems that to become a Catholic is to put on an intellectual straitjacket. Not so. It is no restraint on liberty of opinion to insist that there is such a thing as objective truth, or to believe and teach that truth in all its fullness. St Augustine, as ever, put it best when he said, 'In essentials, unity; where there is doubt, liberty; in all things, charity.' That remains the Catholic ideal.

Is my path, as I have tried to describe it in this essay, the only way into the Church? No, of course not. There are as many ways as there are people. In each person's intellectual and spiritual formation, in the events and circumstances of his or her life, there will be opportunities to encounter Jesus of Nazareth and the Church he founded. It is a matter of being open, vigilant and alert to those opportunities; and of not squandering them through inattention or foreclosing them by an *a priori* assumption of dogmatic materialism.

Several people may arrive at the same conclusion. But that is no proof that they arrived at it by the same process of reasoning. In fact, given the complex nature of the illative sense and of religious belief, it is almost inevitable that no two people will ever follow precisely the same heuristic processes. No two people are exactly alike. Any two people, even identical twins, will have somewhat different ideas, different aptitudes, different strengths and weaknesses, different experiences, different formations, different leanings, and so on. This is the chief reason why so much religious discussion is inconclusive. What seems convincing to one person will not seem so to another. Nor need this imply anything about their respective intellects. In terms of intelligence, reasoning ability, impartiality, freedom from bias,[9] knowledge of the relevant facts, they may be identical. Yet they may still arrive at different conclusions, or at the same conclusion for different reasons. Hence the reasons given in defence of the Catholic Faith by Newman, Belloc and Chesterton (to cite just three examples) are not identical. All three were highly intelligent. Newman and Belloc were both Oxford men, and Chesterton, though he never formally attended a university or took a degree, was by no means unlearned or ill-educated. Yet all three had subtly different grounds of belief, as is clearly shown by their respective apologetic writings.

Towards the end of *Orthodoxy*, his 1908 apologetic masterpiece, G. K. Chesterton says, 'I have now said enough to show (to any one to whom such an explanation is essential) that I have in the ordinary arena of apologetics, a ground of belief.' For my part, I hope that I too have said enough to show that I have a reasonable ground of belief – even if it is not one that you, gentle reader, can accept. I also hope that I shall not have deterred anyone from pursuing his own path into the Church, however different it may be from mine. Perhaps because I was raised as a Christian, perhaps because I attended a Catholic school for five years, perhaps because of my reading in Catholic authors, I did not feel as if, by entering the Catholic Church, I had taken my life in a radically new direction. On the contrary, I felt that, like the prodigal son in the parable, I had come home. I had not merely recovered the lost faith of my childhood, but gained something more, something of inexpressible value: a philosophical ground of belief; a balanced, ordered and coherent view of the universe; and a locus of legitimate authority on all matters relating to faith and morals. To borrow some words from Fr Aidan Nichols, I had acquired a wider Christianity than I had previously known and a wider *humanitas* as well. That, surely, is a cause for gratitude.

At the outset of this essay, I undertook to give valid reasons for my conversion to the Catholic Faith. I hope I have fulfilled that promise. But I want to conclude with two quotations that summarize, with a clarity I could never hope to rival, the most compelling reasons for accepting Christian theism, of which the most coherent, persuasive and authoritative form is that embodied in the Catholic Church. The first is from Blessed John Henry Newman—

'Unless we have some just idea of our hearts and of sin, we can have no right idea of a Moral Governor, a Saviour or a Sanctifier [...]. Thus self-knowledge is at the root of all real religious knowledge; and it is in vain – worse than vain – it is a deceit and a mischief, to think to understand the Christian doctrines as a matter of course, merely by being taught by books, or by attending sermons, or by any outward means, however excellent, taken by themselves. For it is in proportion as we search our hearts and understand our own nature, that we understand what is meant by an Infinite Governor and Judge; in proportion as we comprehend the nature of disobedience and our actual sinfulness, that we feel what is the blessing of the removal of sin, redemption, pardon, sanctification, which otherwise are mere words. God speaks to us primarily in our hearts. Self-knowledge is the key to the precepts and doctrines of Scripture. The very utmost any outward notices of religion can do, is to startle us and make us turn inward and search our hearts; and then, when we have experienced what it is to read ourselves, we shall profit by the doctrines of the Church and the Bible.'

And the second is from the sometime Wykeham Professor of Logic at Oxford University, Sir Michael Dummett—

'The most important thing is that it makes sense to talk about doing things for the love of God. Now, it is presumptuous of me to mention such things, but the fact is that the few lives that exemplify something far above the average are the lives that are devoted to the love of God. For the love of God, people do what, from any other standpoint, is throwing away their lives. I'm not talking only about people who risk martyrdom, but [also about those] who give up their whole lives to relieving the suffering of the utterly wretched, or for that matter those who give up their lives to [prayer], penance and contemplation. I don't know anywhere else we can find anything that counterbalances the extremes of human wickedness which very frequently occur. The one thing I feel I cannot do is to adopt a view of the world which would make nonsense of such lives. When it comes to it, that is where my loyalty lies.'

Jon Elsby, February 2013

Epilogue

Epilogue

Advice to Young Catholics

So far, you have read the story of my conversion from atheism to Catholicism. I have stated my ground of belief: the sum total of the considerations that induced me to abandon one set of beliefs about the universe and adopt another. Most of those considerations were experiential, as I found the philosophical arguments inconclusive. But, after all, anyone who reads this will be a different person from me, with different life experiences, and also (perhaps) different pre-rational assumptions about the way in which those experiences should be interpreted and understood. Why should such a person find *my* reasons convincing?

Well, perhaps they will not. Perhaps they will find their own way into the Church, their own reasons to believe. And perhaps their reasons will be very different from mine, and the arguments they find compelling will not be the ones that persuaded me. Arguments and evidence drawn from science, art, jurisprudence, history and philosophy, as well as from the general store of human experience, may lead people into the Church. And, apart from the general store of experience, there is the fact of one's own particular life experience – the people one has known, the places one has lived in, the art one has seen, the music one has heard, and the books one has read. Any of these, or some combination of all of them, might awaken a sense of vocation, of being called into the Church – not necessarily as a priest, but as a believing, practising Catholic Christian. No one should think that the door is locked against him. If the door is locked, it is on the inquirer's side, not that of the Church.

The world today is a very confusing place, especially for the young, who find themselves confronted by a veritable smorgasbord of worldviews, each claiming (at least implicitly) to be in sole possession of the truth, and none of them compatible with any of the others. A young person today has to weigh the conflicting claims of all-embracing belief systems such as existentialism, Marxism, monism, scientific humanism, atheism, agnosticism, behaviourism, materialism, Deism, Gnosticism, Zoroastrianism, Bahaism, Buddhism, Hinduism, Sufism, Islam, Sikhism, Judaism, Protestantism, astrology, occultism, theosophy, and all the Christian heresies, New Age cults and varieties of paganism you can think of. All these, and more, are on offer in the global supermarket of religions and worldviews. And the problems do not end there, because, in addition to the comprehensive belief systems, philosophical positions like determinism, relativism, subjectivism, indifferentism, liberalism, libertinism, hedonism, modernism, utilitarianism and syncretism also have to be considered. Even a young person who has been reared in the Catholic Faith from infancy will face difficult choices when s/he arrives at the age when s/he can think independently.

So young Catholics today face unprecedented challenges. And, quite apart from the bewildering variety of choices on offer, there is the undeniable fact that the prevailing temper of the age is secular, and sceptical in matters of faith. Nor is this a matter of a neutral, philosophical scepticism, for today the sceptical attitude of mind often manifests itself as a violent and visceral hostility to Christianity in general, and to the Catholic Church and her doctrines in particular. Moreover, young Catholics – the children of those brought up since the Second Vatican Council – have often been imperfectly catechized at school and at home, and are, therefore, ill-equipped with reasoned arguments with which to defend the Faith against the assaults of their opponents. Not surprisingly, faced with manifold difficulties arising from all these circumstances, they often either deliberately abandon their Faith, or else just drift away (through inertia rather than conscious choice) and cease to practise. What advice can an older Catholic – one, perhaps, better acquainted with the philosophical and theological basis of Catholic doctrine – offer to his younger co-religionists?

Perhaps something like this—

You stand today on the threshold of your adult lives. Unlimited possibilities, for better or worse, lie before you. Your schooldays are over, and with them, your childhood. 'When I was a child, I spoke as a child, I understood as a child, I thought as a child: but when I became a man, I put away childish things' says St Paul (1 Corinthians 13). You, too, have put away childish things, including the simple faith of your childhood: it is no longer 'fit for purpose', to use a modern phrase. At college or university, you will meet many people who challenge your faith – people perhaps more learned or cleverer than you are, whose ground of belief is different from yours; people of other faiths; people of no faith at all; and people who see faith *per se* as something incompatible with reason and therefore to be attacked. How will you meet their challenges? How will you defend your faith? What ground of belief will *you* have to offer?

External challenges are not the only trials you will face. You will also face trials from within. Your faith will not always be strong. At times, it will be weak and vulnerable. You will meet failure, frustration, disappointment, pain, grief, loss, illness and bereavement. It may be that, at precisely those times, when you most need Him, God will seem absent. You may feel alone and abandoned in a universe that is silent, absurd, without meaning or purpose, indifferent to human pain and suffering. How will you react to this sense of absence, emptiness and abandonment? Will your faith support, encourage and enlighten you? Will it be strengthened by ordeals? Or will it be weakened, perhaps fatally?

Sometimes, too, you will face difficult choices. You will be caught on the horns of a dilemma, the *argumentum cornutum*, where you are forced to choose between what appear to be equally unpalatable alternatives. How – by reference to what criteria – will you choose? Ultimately, will your criteria be moral or practical? Will they be discovered in experience, or invented by you? What effect will being confronted with, and actually making, such choices, have on your faith? Will you be tempted to blame God, to be angry with Him, or to cease to believe in Him, simply because he has set before you hard choices? Will you yield to those temptations? What, if anything, will prevent you from doing so?

I have posed a number of awkward questions for you to consider. But they all have one thing in common: namely, that they require, first and foremost, reasoned answers – that is, answers based on a process of rational argument. Answers based on an unreflective, unexamined faith are nothing to the purpose. It is precisely such faith that is called into question by the challenges I have postulated.

You may think that this sounds a very dry, uninteresting business. What has rational argumentation to do with faith, you may be wondering. Surely faith is not just intellectual? It involves the heart as well as the head – perhaps the heart more than the head. As Pascal says, *Le cœur a ses raisons que la raison ne connaît point*. Faith is feeling as well as thought. After all, Jesus did not choose intellectuals as his disciples. He chose fishermen, a tax collector – in short, ordinary people. They could not *reason* their way to faith, nor were they expected to do so. Why should we?

The answer is that the apostles did not need rational argument. They had before them the tremendous and tangible fact of Christ. They had their own direct, unmediated experience of his presence and his teaching. We do not. Our experience of Christ is mediated by scripture, by the sacraments, and by the Church. If our faith is not supported by reasons, it will be fragile. When tested, it may fail, leaving us rudderless and bereft of any guiding principle. That is why we need reasons to believe. Our faith must be underpinned by reason and evidence because they are necessary to its survival.

How, then, should we go about supporting our faith with reasons? I have eight suggestions for you to consider—

1 *Take every opportunity to grow in knowledge and understanding of the Faith.* Many people adopt atheism as a default position without ever having examined and

compared the truth claims of the Catholic Faith with those of atheism. That is a lazy way of thinking – or, rather, it is a way of avoiding having to think. As a faithful Catholic, you should read Scripture every day by studying the daily readings in the Missal; say the morning and evening prayers prescribed by the Divine Office; attend Mass on all holy days of obligation; study the Catechism often; and examine your conscience daily. Remember: bad habits corrode virtues; good habits form them.

2 *For every book you read by a non-Catholic, make sure you read one by a Catholic author.* By the term 'Catholic author', I don't mean an author who just happens incidentally to be a Catholic. I mean a writer who either tackles specifically Catholic themes, or writes about general themes from a specifically Catholic standpoint. Such writers may be poets, novelists, essayists, satirists, social or cultural critics, historians, theologians, philosophers, playwrights – what you will. The important thing is that they should write as proponents of orthodox Catholic belief. It is also worth remembering that the CTS (Catholic Truth Society) offers a wide range of doctrinally sound, cogently argued, inexpensive publications by major Catholic authors and thinkers. They deserve close attention.

3 *If someone raises any objections to the Catholic Church or to the substance of the Catholic Faith that you have not previously considered, find out the relevant facts before*

attempting a response. Don't be afraid to admit ignorance – but, having admitted it, seek the remedy. Check the historical records. See what the Catechism says. Look up any references to Scripture. Make sure you know not only exactly what the Church teaches on the subject in question, but also the reasons why she teaches it. This is especially necessary where the subject is controversial. Then you may consider whether – and, if so, to what extent – the objections advanced really stand up to rational scrutiny.

4 *Read the Fathers and Doctors of the Church.* They will help you to interpret Scripture and the Church's Tradition correctly. Study theologians, philosophers and devotional writers who are broadly orthodox in belief. Read Papal encyclicals and other official Church documents. Read thinkers like Augustine, Aquinas, Pascal and Newman. Read the most engaging apologists for Christian orthodoxy – i.e. a version of Christianity, whether Catholic or not, that is grounded in Scripture and tradition. They include G. K. Chesterton, Hilaire Belloc, Ronald Knox, C. S. Lewis and Dorothy L. Sayers.

5 *Own a good library of Catholic books.* Minimally, you should own a Catholic Bible and the Sunday Missal. A Weekday Missal, a Catholic Commentary on Holy Scripture, the Catechism of the Catholic Church, the Compendium of the Social Doctrine of the Church, the Shorter Morning and Evening Prayer, and a general Catholic Dictionary are also useful, as are Catholic

reference works on the Bible, theology and the liturgy.
You should also own a good basic exposition of the
Catholic Faith. There are several to choose from. Ronald
Knox's *The Belief of Catholics*, A. N. Gilbey's *We Believe*,
Robert Barron's *Catholicism*, and Alban McCoy's *An
Intelligent Person's Guide to Catholicism* may all be
highly recommended, and there are many others. Keep
all these books to hand; read and consult them
frequently.

6 *Remember that the Church is older and wiser than you or
her critics.* Her teaching has endured and evolved over
2,000 years. Her dogmas have not been arbitrarily
dreamt up by any one person, but have been laboriously
hammered out in conciliar discussions and theological
debates in response to the most pressing exigencies, and
in order to avert the twin dangers of falling into heresy
or schism. She numbers among her saints and sages
some of the greatest and wisest men and women who
have ever lived. So you should follow the old Catholic
maxim, *sentire cum ecclesia* – think with the Church. Do
not be too ready to agree with her detractors or to accept
their arguments simply because they happen to be currently fashionable.

7 *Don't just read about your Faith – practise it.* A belief that
is purely intellectual and does not issue in action is inau-
thentic and falls far short of the faith demanded by
Christ: the faith of the apostles, saints and martyrs.
Theirs was a faith in which belief and action were insepa-

rable. The only purpose of reading about the Faith and growing in understanding of it, is that, having done so, you will know how to live and act in the world. You will be able to see the proper relations between prayer and praxis, or, to put it another way, between Church and charity. Armed with that understanding, you will be better able to live out your faith in spite of ridicule, opposition, or persecution.

8 *Remember that, for the Christian, action includes prayer.* Christianity is not reducible to social work. Nor is it a department of sociology, anthropology, psychotherapy, or self-actualization. It is, first and foremost, the truth about humankind, our place in the universe, and the relations that properly subsist between us and our neighbour and God. So, for the Christian, right action is not confined to helping others. It also entails an active life of prayer, meditation and worship; and these imperatives must not be neglected any more than the imperatives to love your neighbour and do good to those that hate you.

If you follow these suggestions, I am confident that you will grow in faith and understanding, and that you will be able to defend the Church and refute the arguments of her critics.

Perhaps you think that what I am advocating is not reasoned thought but sheer indoctrination. Isn't the primary object of higher education to teach you, not *what* to think, but *how* to think for yourself? What I have proposed, you might say, is the diametric opposite of free and independent thought. It is nothing less than brainwashing, designed to achieve slavish conformity to the dictates of the Church, many of which are as unreasonable as her detractors claim.

There are three points to make in response to this. First, *reasoned thought* and *free and independent thought* are not necessarily the same thing. Any attempt to draw a facile equation between them, or – what is more likely – any careless blurring of the distinction between them, should be strongly resisted. Reasoned thought must be free and independent; but free and independent thought is not necessarily reasonable. From the fact that a thought or belief is original, and has been freely arrived at, nothing follows as to its rational justification. By the same token, a belief may be 'authentic' (to use the jargon of existentialism) – which is to say, it may be sincerely, and strongly, held – but it is not on that account necessarily true. Conformity to the Church's teaching is not irrational if one is both convinced on the evidence, and entitled to be so convinced, that her teaching is true.

Second, bear in mind the context in which I offer this advice. We live in a secular culture, one in which religious voices are often mocked, marginalized, or even excluded from the public square. The mass media are resolutely committed to secularism. So are most of the institutes of higher education. And so, it seems, are the majority of our politicians, irrespective of what party they belong to. All the churches, including the Catholic Church, are battling against a process of attrition caused, at least in part, by the secularization of society, and symptomized by ageing and dwindling congregations. Young people often drift away, not from conviction, or because, by any severe effort at reasoned thought, they have been persuaded that the Church's teachings are false, but rather because they are more susceptible to influence from the media, the fashion industry, popular culture, advertisers and contemporaries – in short, from the prevailing *Zeitgeist* – than from the Church. In such a context, to preserve and support a Faith – even one which we are convinced, on rational grounds, is the truth – is far from easy. It is much easier to 'go with the flow', to give up thinking, to accept uncritically the opinions of the majority, and to abandon views that are unpopular in order to be 'in the swim'. For the present, the real danger of indoctrination comes from the dominant secularism of the culture, rather than from the Church. Faith is simply not given a fair hearing.

Third, remember that faith is a supernatural gift, not something we have earned, or to which we have a right. Like all such gifts, it must be received with gratitude to the Giver and with a firm resolve to hold and preserve it. That means taking responsibility for it, nurturing it, and enabling it to grow in spite of the unfavourable political, social, moral and intellectual environment. The parable of the sower and the seed teaches us that faith will not flourish in poor ground, or in unpropitious circumstances. Now, we are free to choose whether to coöperate with God in nurturing this gift of faith or not. We can accept His gift, treasure it and tend it carefully. Or we can reject it, ignore it and treat it with contempt. We are not compelled to choose one way or the other. But, in Blessed John Henry Newman's words, *We can believe what we choose. We are answerable for what we choose to believe.* And what we choose to believe, and how we treat the gift of faith, will determine not only how we live, but also whether, when we most need it, we shall have any faith to draw on or not.

†

Does it matter what we believe? Many people would say that it doesn't. What matters, according to them, is how we behave. We can believe whatever we like so long as our beliefs remain private and we act in the public square as good citizens – earning a living, keeping the laws, paying our taxes, treating other people fairly, and so on. Provided we do those things, it doesn't matter whether we are Christians, Mormons, Muslims, Marxists, Moonies, or members of the Monster Raving Loony Party. What is the problem with that?

Well, the main problem is that it's nonsense. Beliefs, if they are sincerely held, cannot remain private. They are motives for action. Beliefs and behaviour act upon each other, so that we behave according to our beliefs, which are then reinforced by our behavioural praxis.

With that in mind, consider the main differences between a Christian view of the world and a purely secular one, using the table as reference on the facing page. Does it seem likely that the people who accept the secular worldview will be motivated to behave like the people who accept the Christian worldview? Hardly! What, for example, would a secularist who had enough respect for logical consistency to ensure that his morals reflected his metaphysics, think about abortion? Or euthanasia? Or infanticide in cases where the newborn was severely disabled, or suffering from an incurable and fatal condition?

What could a secularist say to a libertine who rejected morals altogether? What arguments could he adduce to persuade such a man that it was better to accept a moral code even in the absence of an objective moral law?

CHRISTIAN WORLDVIEW	SECULAR WORLDVIEW
There exists a God who is the Creator and Sustainer of all that exists, the supreme Source of all truth, goodness, wisdom and beauty.	No God exists. The universe and all that is in it are the outcomes of chance. Truth is simply what works in practice. Goodness is a human construct. Wisdom is the power to distinguish between fact and falsehood. Beauty is in the eye of the beholder.
Because God is perfectly good, He desires what conduces to human flourishing. It makes sense therefore to conform one's own will to the Will of God. God's Will is known to us through the Scriptures; the life, teaching, death and resurrection of Jesus Christ; and the teaching of the Church.	Because there is no God, what conduces to human flourishing must be determined by human beings alone. There is no Will superior to the human will, no Reason superior to human reason.
Man is made in the image of God. All human life therefore possesses a sacred and inviolable dignity.	Human life is simply the outcome of blind evolution. Man is a naked ape.
Man is separated from God by some aboriginal catastrophe known in Christian theology as 'Original Sin'. But the separation has never been total because of God's grace. This accounts for Man's dual nature: an orientation towards sin because he prefers his own will to the Will of God, and a Godward orientation because of God's grace.	Sin is a theological fiction. Man is an animal capable of both good and bad actions. But good and evil are whatever human beings decide they are.
God became incarnate in Jesus of Nazareth, the Second Person of the Holy Trinity. In the person of Jesus, we literally encounter God Himself.	Jesus of Nazareth (if he existed) was an itinerant teacher of a kind common in the Middle East in his day. He may have been a good man but was not otherwise remarkable. The Church is built on a lie.
The saints and martyrs are examples of holiness and heroic virtue for Christians to follow.	Many of the saints are not very admirable. St Thomas More, for example, persecuted so-called heretics. There are better examples to follow.
Ethics consists primarily in the practice of virtue and the avoidance of sin. The basis for ethics is our knowledge of the revealed Will of God.	Ethics consists primarily in helping and not harming other people. The basis for ethics is [our intuitive knowledge of right and wrong] [our need for peaceful co-existence] [our human laws and rules] [our subjective preferences] – (delete inapplicable alternatives).
The Four Last Things that we should keep ever before us are Death, Judgment, Heaven and Hell. Death is not final.	There is no judgment. There are no rewards for the virtuous or punishments for the wicked. Death is annihilation.

And the same applies, *mutatis mutandis*, to people who believe in religions other than Christianity. For example, Jews and Muslims accept the *lex talionis*: 'an eye for an eye, and a tooth for a tooth'. For Christians, this has been superseded by the law of charity: the commands to love our neighbour and pray for our enemies. Again, different beliefs will, in certain circumstances, issue in very different courses of action. The view that beliefs don't matter, and that they can somehow be confined to the private sphere, is therefore false.

If beliefs matter, then it also matters that our beliefs should be true and that we should be able to defend them. I have already stated what I believe and my ground of belief. What I am concerned with here is not the propositional content of our beliefs, or the reasons we have for holding them, but the methods by which those beliefs should be defended and attacks on them rebutted.

Where, then, should we start? Where better than with the arguments most likely to be advanced by our opponents?

1 The first argument you are likely to encounter is this—

Look at the sex abuse scandal, and at the way the Church authorities tried to cover it up and protect the offending priests. They did nothing to help the victims until the scandal was exposed. And even then they prevaricated and failed to coöperate with the enquiries by secular authorities. That looks like a powerful human institution acting to protect its worldly interests, not like the Church of Christ. And if the Church didn't require priests to be celibate in the first place, sexual abuse wouldn't occur.

What can we say in response to this? First, we must admit that the scandal of clerical sex abuse is a very grave one. There is no denying the heinousness of the offences or the fact that some bishops and other church officials acted wrongly in treating the offences as sins rather than as crimes. But it must be pointed out that the bishops, for the most part, acted in good faith. They genuinely saw the offenders as sinners, not as criminals. They did not understand, and, at the time when most of these offences were committed, had no reason to suppose, that many paedophiles are manipulative sexual predators with a strong disposition to reoffend. Had they understood this, they would have acted differently. Second, it is still the case that most abuse occurs within the family. The incidence of abuse among the clergy is no higher than it is among the generality of the population: if anything, it is somewhat lower. It is also no higher than it is among the clergy of other churches, whose clergy are allowed to marry. This disproves the contention that clerical sex abuse is causally connected with the requirement of celibacy. Third, an allegation is not proof. Abuse may be wrongly alleged against priests, by accusers acting from malice, or from mercenary motives. Allegations require careful investigation, especially when they relate to offences long past, and are made against priests who have died and cannot defend themselves. Fourth, even if the worst of what is alleged against priests and the Church were true, it would not affect the claims of the Church. The Church claims only infallibility in her teaching on matters relating to faith and morals. She does not claim that she will always be led wisely or intelligently, or that every action of her priests and bishops will be defensible. That all human beings, including popes and priests, sin – sometimes grievously – may be news to the media: it will not be news to the Church.

2 Here is another argument you are likely to encounter—

The Pope is directly responsible for the spread of HIV/AIDS in Africa and for the thousands of deaths that have resulted. If he permitted the use of condoms, HIV and other sexually transmitted diseases would not be spread so widely and would be easier to control.

First, the Pope cannot overturn what the Church has authoritatively taught: he has not the power to do so. Secondly, the Church's teaching on sexual ethics does not only prohibit the use of contraceptives. It also requires fidelity within monogamous marriage and expressly forbids all forms of extra-marital sexual intercourse. If these requirements were universally accepted and acted upon, HIV/AIDS and all other sexually transmitted diseases would never have arisen in the first place, and would be stamped out very quickly even now, when they have arisen. On what grounds, then, can either the Pope or the Church be held responsible for the spread of such diseases?

To clarify this point, let us take an analogy: suppose you seek my advice on investments and I tell you that you will make a good profit if you sell your shares in *x* and buy shares in *y* to an equivalent value. Suppose you later come to me and say that you have followed my advice but have made no profit. I ask whether you sold all your shares in *x* and you say you have. I then ask whether you used the proceeds to buy shares in *y*, and you admit that you did not. I then say to you, 'Well, you followed only half my advice, not the whole of it. I promised you a profit if you did all that I advised. Don't blame me if you did just half of it and have reaped no reward.'

Here our detractor may shift the ground of his argument. The requirement for strict celibacy outside marriage is unrealistic, he will say. All the evidence shows that male sexual urges cannot be repressed. They require gratification; and men will seek such gratification through either sexual liaisons or, if all else fails, through rape. In such circumstances, to allow the use of condoms is the only realistic way to prevent the spread of HIV.

This argument rests on a false premiss. Male sexual urges cannot be *repressed*, but certainly can be *controlled*, and there is a wealth of empirical evidence to prove as much. Most priests and religious lead contented and celibate lives. In the secular world, not all bachelors are rapists or fornicators. Many lead morally blameless lives, and manage to control their sexual appetites while remaining happy and well-adjusted in their relations with others. When all is said and done, we are all free agents and responsible morally and legally for our actions.

3 Some people may use an argument along these lines against the Church—

The Church's ban on remarriage after divorce is unreasonable. In the days when that policy was decided on, rates of mortality and especially the incidence of death in childbirth, ensured that few marriages lasted longer than sixteen years. Now marriages may last much longer. It is only natural that, over time, people will change and may grow apart. With the best will in the world, provision must be made for couples to divorce and remarry – within the Church if they so wish.

The Church's doctrine on marriage is not arbitrary, neither is it merely a policy. It is grounded in the scriptural teaching that marriage is 1) a sacrament, and 2) a covenant: that is, on the one hand, a visible sign of grace, and, on the other, a contract or promise made between a man and a woman, and intended to provide the best and most stable possible framework for the rearing of children. It is not primarily a matter of falling in love: we all know that human emotions are unstable and fickle. People who marry should see the maintenance of their marriage chiefly as a matter of keeping their promises. We all regard keeping promises as self-evidently better than breaking them. That is one of the most basic tenets of ethics. And no more solemn or binding promises can be made than those made in the nuptial Mass. A parish priest will give instruction to young people who intend to marry. He will make sure that they understand that marriage is a lifelong commitment, not something to be undertaken lightly or for frivolous reasons. No one is saying that marriage is easy. It needs work and genuine commitment by both parties. And, in spite of everything they can do, it may break down. But not even the Church has the authority to alter a sacrament ordained by Christ himself.

4 What about arguments from history? Here are four of the most common—

The Crusades were brutal wars of Christian aggression aimed at enriching the Church and extending her sphere of power and influence. How does this square with Christian moral teaching or with the Church's claim to be the Body of Christ on earth?

The Spanish Inquisition tortured and murdered, by burning and garrotting, thousands of so-called heretics, with the Pope's approval. It was the worst and most terrifying instrument of ecclesiastical oppression ever devised. How can that be reconciled with the idea of an infallible Church?

The Church silenced Galileo and forced him under extreme duress to recant a scientific hypothesis that was subsequently verified. How can that be reconciled with the idea of an infallible Church?

Pope Pius XII has been called Hitler's Pope. He refused to speak out against the Nazis, to condemn the genocide of the Jews or the persecution of political opponents. Is this conduct worthy of the Vicar of Christ?

All these arguments can be convincingly rebutted. But before we consider them individually, I shall suggest a general methodological approach to arguments of this kind.

In all these cases, acquaint yourself first with all the
relevant historical facts. When you read history, take care
to distinguish proven fact from authorial opinion. Ask
yourself what the author's point of view is, and what his
motives are. Is he impartial? Or, conversely, is he notably
pro- or anti-Catholic? Is he rigorous in his methods of
inquiry? Does he cite his sources? If so, how reliable are
they? How reliable is *he* as a source of information? Is he
selective or comprehensive in his presentation of
evidence? Does he interrogate all the available sources?
Does he seek confirmation and corroboration of his
judgments? Does he account adequately for disconfirming
evidence? Are his inferences warranted by the data from
which they are drawn, or does he (sometimes?
persistently?) go beyond what the data support? Have you
yourself got access to first-hand sources? If so, have you
consulted them? Distinguish between strong and weak
evidence, and hold opinions only as firmly as the totality
of the evidence warrants.

Make sure that you read at least some of the Catholic
historians, such as Hilaire Belloc, Christopher Dawson,
Philip Hughes, Paul Johnson, Michael Walsh, Lucy
Beckett and Eamon Duffy, especially if you have already
read non- or anti-Catholic historians such as Carlyle,
Macaulay, Trevelyan, or, in modern times, Sir Steven
Runciman, A. J. P. Taylor and Daniel Goldhagen. A useful
starting point is Belloc's admirable short work, *The
Catholic Church and History*. His *Europe and the Faith* and
The Crisis of Our Civilization are also valuable.

Now let's consider the arguments enumerated above.

We haven't the space to treat them in detail: a few brief remarks must suffice to indicate the general direction of further research and inquiries. So, taking them in the order shown—

The Crusades The history of the Crusades is complex, and to ascribe them to a single motive or to lay all the responsibility on the Church, is misleading. They involved not only Christians and Muslims, but pagans and heretics. The early Crusades were a response to Muslim aggression and expansion. Their purpose was, first, to recapture Christian lands that had been lost to Muslim invaders; and, secondly, to deter those invaders from attempting further incursions into Christendom. That the wars were brutal (as wars tend to be by their very nature) is undeniable; but the brutality was on both sides. It was not an effect of the precepts of Christianity or of the teaching of the Church. The Church's claim to be the sole custodian of divinely revealed truth is not affected by anything that happened during the course of the Crusades. Whether that claim is valid or invalid must be decided on other grounds.

It is instructive to consider what the subsequent history of Europe might have been if the Crusades had not been fought. Spain had fallen to the Moors, and Italy was menaced; nor does it seem likely that Muslim expansionism would have ended there. If Europe had been converted to Islam, it is hard to see how the principles of liberal democracy would ever have taken root there. Islam has no doctrine of the separation of spiritual and temporal powers such as Christianity has ('Render unto Caesar the things that are Caesar's and unto God the things that are God's'); and that doctrine made possible the gradual development of democratic institutions. An Islamic Europe composed of theocratic states would have had a very different history and culture.

As to war, it is true that no war can easily be reconciled with Christian moral teaching. Nevertheless, it should be remembered, first, that Christianity does not entail pacifism; and, second, that of all religions and worldviews, only Christianity has made a conscientious attempt to mitigate and place limits upon the brutality of war. The basic principles of just war doctrine were first articulated by St Augustine and subsequently enlarged upon by St Thomas Aquinas and others. They remain valid to this day. That doctrine has ensured (so far as such a thing can be ensured) that wars are no more cruel and inhuman than they have to be. The principles of just war doctrine, which are described as 'the conditions for legitimate defence by military force', are—

1 The damage inflicted on the nation or community of nations must be lasting, grave and certain.
2 All other means of putting an end to it must have been shown to be impractical or ineffective.
3 There must be a serious prospect of success.
4 The use of arms must not produce evils and disorders greater than the evil to be eliminated.

If these principles are applied to the Crusades, it is at least arguable that all the conditions for a just war were met.

The Spanish Inquisition The Spanish Inquisition was a tool of political oppression instituted by the Spanish Crown. Throughout its history, from its establishment in 1481 until its dissolution in 1834, it was under the direct control not of the Church, but of the Spanish monarchy. It is true that the Spanish Inquisition engaged in abominable practices, such as the use of torture to extract 'confessions' from supposed heretics, and the burning and garrotting of those deemed its enemies. No sane person would wish to defend such practices today. But I repeat: the Spanish Inquisition was an instrument of the Spanish Crown whose purpose was to augment political control and authority, and weaken opposition.

The Spanish Inquisition should not be confused with the Roman Inquisition, which is now known as the Congregation for the Doctrine of the Faith (or CDF for short). The Roman Inquisition was also a feared institution, and it also engaged in practices that would be regarded today as unacceptable – even barbaric. At that period in history, the Church's view of heresy was that 'error had no rights'. This view has changed. Since the Second Vatican Council (1962–65), non-Catholic Christians have been referred to not as 'heretics' but as 'separated brethren' – a more eirenic term – and dialogue has been encouraged rather than forbidden.

The actions of the Inquisition, however reprehensible, do not bear upon the infallibility of the Church. The doctrine of infallibility is extremely complex and subtle, and has been the subject of innumerable theological essays, including some of book length. It is also one of the principal stumbling blocks to anyone approaching the Church for the first time, so it is important that you, as believing Catholics, should understand it and be able to defend it.

The first thing to say is that the Church's claim to infallibility is grounded in the promises of Christ recorded in Scripture[10] and on what follows logically from the acceptance of those promises. It is important to insist on this. Those who dispute the point should be asked, first, how they think those promises are to be interpreted if they do not constitute a guarantee of infallibility addressed specifically to St Peter and his successors, and, more generally, to the whole Church; and, secondly, what authority they have for their interpretation.

What does it mean to say that the Church is infallible? It does not mean that individual Popes, bishops and priests will never make mistakes. What it does mean is that, because of the guidance of the Holy Spirit, the Church cannot teach error in matters of faith or morals. The infallibility of the Church is ordinarily expressed in the common teaching of her bishops; in the decisions of Ecumenical Councils on points of doctrine; and (very occasionally) in decisions made by the Pope outside a Council but in consultation with the other bishops. That, in brief, is the Catholic doctrine of infallibility.

One can see that the doctrine of infallibility, and the concomitant view that there exist such things as objective truth and a locus of legitimate authority in religion, are profoundly dissonant with almost universally accepted features of the modern worldview such as democracy, subjectivism, relativism and liberalism. The Church is already under immense pressure, not all of it originating in external sources, to abandon her historic teaching and embrace the modernist worldview. However, were she to do so, she would cease to exist. It is essential to her survival, and to her maintenance of her historic identity and mission, that she does not fall into the manifold errors of modernism, even if this means that she suffers persecution and/or an enormous reduction in numbers, resources and practical efficacy. To place short-term practical results before her timeless witness to the truth would be fatal. A Christian, of course, must place entire confidence in the promises of Christ in this as in all other matters.

The doctrine of infallibility, perhaps together with the doctrine of transubstantiation, is probably the most often cited reason Christians of other denominations find it impossible to become Catholics. The argument generally runs like this—

1 No individual or institution can validly claim infallibility.
2 All institutions possess imperatives to preserve and
   enhance their power.
3 The doctrine of infallibility is a clear instance of such an
   imperative in action.
4 Therefore the doctrine is false.

Put like that, the argument is clearly not just formally invalid but logically incoherent. It begins with an unexamined dogmatic assumption – that no individual or institution can validly claim infallibility. Thence it proceeds to a second such assumption – that all institutions possess imperatives to preserve and enhance their power – which does not follow from the first. It then proceeds to a third assumption – that the doctrine of infallibility is a clear instance of such an imperative in action – which does not follow from either of the others. Finally, on the basis of three logically unconnected assumptions, which we are apparently required to accept as axiomatic, it concludes that the doctrine of infallibility is false! Is there any other subject on which intelligent people would advance such a tissue of *non sequiturs* as a proof?

Suppose we revise the argument and present it as follows—

1 No individual or institution can validly claim infallibility.
2 The Catholic Church claims to be infallible in its teaching on faith and morals.
3 That claim is necessarily false as it violates the first premiss.

There are two points that a Catholic may fairly make in reply. First, the opening premiss is advanced as an axiom without a vestige of proof. Why should it be accepted? Second, the Catholic Church claims only a qualified, not a general, infallibility. Specifically, she claims infallibility for her teaching on faith and morals, and further claims that this infallibility is guaranteed by the promises of Christ recorded in Scripture. Now it is, of course, open to anyone to disbelieve those promises. But then they must answer the question Jesus put to the Pharisees in Matthew 22: 42: *what is your opinion concerning Christ?* Do you think he was just a moral teacher? That is not what he claimed to be. He claimed to be the Christ, the Son of God, the Way, the Truth and the Life. If his claims are false, then we can have no reason for following Christ: why follow someone who was either a liar or deluded? If his claims are true, then his promises are to be believed, for they come from God Himself, the source of all truth.

If the doctrine of infallibility is to be considered impartially on its merits, it is necessary to inquire into the precise nature of the claim, thus—

1 What are the scope and limits of the Church's claimed infallibility: by whom is it exercised, on what occasions (when), through what mechanisms (how), for what purpose (why), over what objects, and with what authority (where is the locus of authority)?
2 On what grounds is the claim to infallibility (however qualified) made?
3 Do the grounds adequately support belief in the doctrine?

Only when these questions have been dispassionately considered and fully answered, will it be possible for an honest inquirer to deliver a verdict on the Church's claim.

Galileo The case of Galileo has often been misrepresented, though a commendably clear account of the facts may be found in Belloc's *The Catholic Church and History*. The main allegations, which have been constantly repeated, are—

1 that Galileo discovered and produced an incontrovertible physical proof of the motion of the earth;
2 that he was condemned by the Catholic Church for stating that proof publicly; and
3 that the Church's condemnation remained in force until the nineteenth century, when she was finally obliged, through sheer embarrassment, to allow the matter to lapse.

These allegations rest upon two erroneous suppositions: first, that Galileo was condemned for teaching what was at that time a new doctrine that he had proved to be true; and secondly, that the Catholic Church in the seventeenth century taught, by her infallible authority as a point of doctrine, that the earth did not move. The facts are as follows—

1 that Galileo had not demonstrated the truth of his hypothesis (which contained a good deal of falsehood as well as a kernel of truth) and was unable to do so during his trial;
2 that the condemnation was against the teaching of an unproven hypothesis as an established fact, not against the hypothesis *per se*;
3 that the condemnation proceeded not from the Catholic Church, but from a particular disciplinary organ of the

Church (the Inquisition), which had no authority to establish a point in doctrine, so the claim that the dispute between Galileo and the Church turned upon a point of authoritative Church teaching is false; and

4 that the theory that the earth turned on its axis and orbited the sun was taught, with the approval of the Church, in Catholic universities as an hypothesis (not as a fact) both before, and after, Galileo's trial.

It is also the case that Galileo, a notoriously prickly and contumacious character, did everything in his power to provoke the Church authorities. The extent to which he was the author of his own downfall is too often forgotten.

All that said, the Galileo case was clearly one – and by no means the only one – where the Inquisition, as the Church's principal disciplinary organ, acted with undue harshness and severity. The slowness of the ecclesiastical authorities to acknowledge this and make what reparation they could, is regrettable and has done great damage to the Church's standing.

Pope Pius XII The reputation of Pius XII has suffered because of his alleged failure to speak out against the atrocities perpetrated by the Nazis, in particular the Holocaust. That he was personally involved in the rescue of some 5,000 Roman Jews, who were hidden in Vatican territory, has not prevented his detractors from labelling him an anti-Semite or Hitler's Pope: a grossly defamatory verdict that no honest person who has troubled to acquaint himself with the facts could possibly endorse.

Pius faced a hideous dilemma. If he spoke out explicitly condemning the Nazis, Catholics in Germany and elsewhere in territories under Nazi control might have suffered the consequences. So might the Jews concealed in the Vatican and others under the protection of the Church. Moreover, Pius repeatedly told the allied leaders that he could denounce Nazi crimes only if he also denounced Soviet crimes. It is hard to take issue with the logic of this.

In the event, the nearest Pius came to an unequivocal condemnation of the Nazis' murderous policies was a statement towards the end of his Christmas Eve broadcast of 1942, in which he lamented the fate of 'hundreds of thousands, who, through no fault of their own, and sometimes only because of their nationality or race, have been consigned to death or slow decline'. In a recent book,[11] Professor Eamon Duffy comments: 'There was no explicit mention of either Jews or Germans.[12] For the rest of his life the Pope believed that this coded utterance was an unequivocal and outspoken condemnation of Nazi genocide against the Jews. Few people then or since have agreed.' Duffy concludes that, while Pius was not an anti-Semitic monster, 'in the face of one of the most terrible crimes in human history, impartial diplomacy and agonized calculation do not seem an adequate response from Christ's vicar on earth. While the helpless were being slaughtered, the most powerful voice in Christendom faltered, and fell silent.' Many will agree. But then hindsight is always 20/20. What is indisputable is that a man reticent by nature, scholarly by inclination, and a diplomat by training, was disqualified by all three to handle the dilemma posed by totalitarian state-imposed terror otherwise than as he did. Pius emerges from an impartial examination of his motives (so far as they may be inferred) as a tragic figure: a highly intelligent and profoundly good man who did his best in an appalling situation, but who was unable to display qualities of boldness and leadership that were simply not his to command.

It is only fair to point out that, if the Pope had displayed those qualities, and millions of Catholics had perished as a result, the indictment against him today, by critics who bear no responsibilities and are always wise after the event, would be no less severe.

As far as the Catholic Church as a whole is concerned, it must also be pointed out that, as early as 10 March 1937, Pius XII's predecessor, Pope Pius XI, had issued the encyclical *Mit brennender Sorge* ('With burning concern'), addressed to the Church in Germany, in which he criticized Nazism, its racial doctrines, and its idolatry of the state, as well as mounting a vigorous defence of the Old Testament. Arguably, the encyclical did not go far enough, and was couched in excessively cautious terms. But how many other organizations were comparably outspoken in their criticisms of the Nazis as early as 1937? Even in September 1938, the British and French governments were still seeking an agreement with the Nazi government of Germany, and were ready to settle for one procured at the cost of their own honour. In that context, Pius XI's encyclical seems a courageous and principled act of defiance: an instance of the Church speaking truth to power.

5 Atheistic philosophers have adduced many arguments against theism. One common philosophical argument, directed specifically against Christian theism, runs like this—

The Christian concept of God is formed by taking three propositions in conjunction, viz. 1) God is all-powerful. 2) God is all-benevolent. 3) There is much suffering (or pain or evil) in the world. If God were all-powerful and suffering existed, He would not be all-benevolent. If God were all-benevolent and suffering existed, He would not be all-powerful. And if God were all-powerful and all-benevolent, suffering would not exist. Therefore the Christian concept of God is a contradiction in terms: He does not, and cannot, exist. In technical terms, He is logically incapable of instantiation.

The argument rests on a false conception of omnipotence. To say that God is omnipotent does not mean that He can do anything at all. It does not mean, for example, that He can create a square circle, or an object that is red all over and blue all over at the same time, or a universe in which 2 + 2 = 5. It means that God can do anything that is *logically* possible. There is a distinction between logical and empirical possibility. It is an empirical impossibility for a man to run from Oxford to London in five minutes, but it is not logically impossible because it does not involve a contradiction in terms. A square circle is a logical impossibility because it *does* involve a contradiction in terms: the properties of squareness and circularity are mutually exclusive; no one object can therefore possess them both. God, being omnipotent, can do anything that is logically possible, including things that are beyond the capability of any created being (that is to say, things that are empirically impossible). But not even omnipotence can do that which is logically (or intrinsically) impossible.

Now, suppose God wished, for His own reasons, to create a world of beings made in His own image – that is, of free, intelligent and rational beings. It is at least moderately probable that a loving God would wish to create such a world because its creation would involve bringing into being a new kind of good. However, in order to create such a world, He would have to create one in which 1) those beings were free to choose between good and evil, and 2) good and ill fortune were distributed randomly, rather than in the form of rewards for the virtuous and punishments for the wicked. To suppose otherwise would be to suppose God able to do the logically impossible, viz. to create a world in which a) free, intelligent and rational beings were able freely to choose between good and evil, and b) causes of volition were pre-ordained, making freedom of choice impossible. Therefore the argument fails.

In order to refute the argument against the Christian God stated above, you need go no further. All that is needed is a narrative that may be true for all anyone knows, and in which the existence of suffering and the existence of an all-powerful, all-benevolent God are logically reconciled. However, if you want to present positive arguments for God's existence that are indicative but not probative, and that depend solely on natural reason and not on divine revelation, then look at the Five

Ways of St Thomas Aquinas. The argument from contingency is especially persuasive (or so it seems to me). Other well-known philosophical arguments that have been advanced over the years with varying degrees of success in order to 'prove' the existence of God (or, at least, to demonstrate that the hypothesis that God exists is more reasonable than any alternative) are the *ontological argument* of St Anselm, Pascal's *Wager* (not an argument as such, but certainly an interesting line of apologetic reasoning), the *argument from natural sufficiency* of C. S. Lewis, and the *argument from proper basicality* of Alvin Plantinga.

†

I have outlined here some of the commoner objections to the Church and the Catholic Faith, and suggested possible responses. However, this account is not exhaustive. There are many other questions that may be raised and objections that may be advanced. For a fuller account, see *What is Catholicism?* by Fr John Redford[13] and *Objections to Roman Catholicism* by Michael de la Bedoyere – both excellent reference works that deal with the main issues in greater detail than I have been able to in this short essay, and provide cogent answers to them.

What I have sketched here, and what is more substantively offered in the books I have mentioned, is not faith but merely a rational foundation on which faith may be built. Faith, as Newman said, involves an assent of the will as well as of the intellect. It requires an unreserved commitment of the whole human person – heart and mind, body and soul, will and intellect.

I have tried to map the route to a faith grounded in reason and oriented towards objective truth.

Whether you take the next steps or not is up to you.

Notes

¹ St Thomas's School in Hildenborough. Sadly, it no longer exists, though the building remains and it is still a school.

² Regrettably, this seems to be an ineradicable trait because it survived both the loss, and subsequently the recovery, of my faith.

³ I don't mean to imply that all Anglo-Saxon philosophers were exponents of linguistic analysis or that all Continental philosophers were phenomenologists: merely that linguistic analysis and phenomenology were, at the time when I first became interested in philosophy, the dominant schools of thought in Britain and Continental Europe respectively.

⁴ In fact, I was wrong. Few of the troubadours were humble travelling musicians. Many were noblemen who remained in one place, perhaps attached to a court, for long periods. Their material ranged from vulgar folksongs to spiritual and metaphysical lyrics of great beauty and refinement. And their vocal technique, however unsophisticated, would have been quite different from that of singers habituated to the use of microphones and artificial amplification. This is an example of how an interesting conclusion can follow from a chain of reasoning based on false premises.

⁵ No doubt that is a dangerous thing to say, suggesting as it

does that I am now too perspicacious to fall into similar errors. In fact, it is possible – even probable – that I am now being equally obtuse in other ways that would seem equally incredible to other people. One should never imagine that one has somehow become more enlightened through one's own endeavours. As far as one's own endeavours are concerned, one remains whatever one has always been. Enlightenment, if it comes at all, comes from without, not within. It is a gift, not a cause for self-congratulation, and it should be received with gratitude, not smugness.

6 Of course, such technology is no longer limited to cinema, radio, the gramophone and television, but now includes videos, DVDs, CDs, personal computers and computer games, laptops, Blackberries, mobile phones, iPods and MP3 players. The situation is therefore immeasurably worse now, in 2015, than it was in the 1970s.

7 And it recalls two other penetrating aphorisms of O'Connor that made an indelible impression on my mind: *The truth does not change according to our ability to stomach it emotionally*, and *To expect too much is to have a sentimental view of life and this is a softness that ends in bitterness.*

8 Gertrud von le Fort invented the central character, Blanche de la Force, whose surname is a Gallicized version of hers. Bernanos added the Old Prioress, who, like him at the time he wrote *Dialogues des Carmélites*, is fifty-nine years old and dying of cancer.

9 Impartiality and freedom from bias are not necessarily the same. Take the case of a judge in an espionage trial. He

may be impartial in the sense of having no prior view as to the guilt or innocence of the accused. But if he regards espionage for foreign powers as a very wicked activity, and if the accused is arguing by way of a defence that, although he is technically guilty, his actions were justified, then the judge, notwithstanding his impartiality in considering the evidence, will have a definite bias against the accused.

[10] 'Thou art Peter and on this rock I will build my Church…and the gates of hell will not prevail against it…I will give you the keys of the kingdom. Whatsoever you bind on earth shall be considered bound in heaven and whatsoever you loose on earth shall be considered loosed in heaven…. Whose sins you forgive, they are forgiven; whose sins you retain, they are retained…. For behold I am with you even to the end of time.'

[11] *Ten Popes Who Shook the World* by Eamon Duffy, Yale University Press and BBC, 2011.

[12] Presumably because the Pope wanted his words to apply equally to Nazi and Soviet atrocities – which indeed they do.

[13] I have given the title of the American edition under which it is also now available in the UK. However, Fr Redford's book was originally published in the UK under the title *Catholicism: Hard Questions*.

Bibliography

W hat follows is a small selection of the books that I either found particularly helpful on my journey from irrational doubt to rational faith, or have found useful since my reception into the Church. They have been helpful for different reasons and in different ways. While the atheist polemics named in the Select Bibliography were helpful because they inadvertently, but conclusively, showed the intellectual lacunae and spiritual inadequacy of the philosophies they were severally seeking to recommend, and the same applies, *mutatis mutandis*, to the works of the more liberal or modernist of the non-Catholic Christians, there were others, of whom T. S. Eliot, C. S. Lewis, Dorothy L. Sayers, David Bentley Hart, and Rowan Williams were the outstanding examples, who were helpful in proving, to my satisfaction, the rationality and coherence of Christian orthodoxy as an explanation of the universe and of our place in it. They thus led me to the threshold of the Church, as it were, without enabling me quite to decide which Church I ought to be received into. Finally, the works of orthodox Catholic authors were helpful because they disclosed to me, for the first time, what I now take, and firmly hold, to be the fullness of truth in matters of faith and morals.

Theologically sophisticated readers (if any!) will note that the writers whose works are listed below differ, sometimes quite radically, about the right way to argue for Christian belief. For example, there is a wide gulf between Richard Swinburne and Alvin Plantinga (both of whom are listed under Suggested Further Reading). They employ different argumentative strategies, the former presenting a probabilistic, cumulative case for the rationality of faith, while the latter argues that belief in God is 'properly basic' – in other words, that it is one of the beliefs we hold about the world which, like belief in the existence of other minds or in the reality of external objects, is so intrinsic to our ability to make sense of the world that we cannot dispense with it without descending into total scepticism. This divergence only proves that, as I have already argued, where the Christian Faith is concerned, there are many routes to the same destination. The existence of other routes need not invalidate the one chosen by a particular writer. And it certainly does not prove that the destination is a chimera.

It will also be noted that the books listed below are of very different types. Some are theological, some philosophical; some are scientific and some autobiographical; some are literary, some are historical; some were written for readers with an academic background, while others were written for a popular audience. The diversity is intentional. It shows that no one, no one at all, is excluded from God's love, mercy, and grace – not even an intellectual!

Select Bibliography

Barth, Karl (1963), *Evangelical Theology: An Introduction*, Grand Rapids: Eerdmans Publishing

Belloc, Hilaire (1921), *Europe and the Faith*, London: Constable

— (1926), *The Catholic Church and History*, New York: The Neumann Press

— (1929), *Survivals and New Arrivals*, London: Sheed & Ward

— (1937), *The Crisis of Our Civilization*, London: Cassell

— (1938), *The Question and the Answer*, London: Longmans, Green & Co Ltd

Benedict XVI, Pope (2007), *Jesus of Nazareth From the Baptism in the Jordan to the Transfiguration*, London: Bloomsbury

— (2011), *Jesus of Nazareth – Holy Week: From the Entrance into Jerusalem to the Resurrection*, London: Catholic Truth Society, San Francisco: Ignatius Press

— (2012), *Jesus of Nazareth: the Infancy Narratives*, London: Bloomsbury

Bernanos, Georges (1952), *Dialogues des Carmélites* (trans *The Fearless Heart*), London: Bodley Head

Boff, Leonardo (1985), *Church, Charism and Power*, London: SCM Press

Bonhoeffer, Dietrich (1937), *The Cost of Discipleship*, London: SCM

— (1953), *Letters and Papers from Prison, London*: SCM

Bultmann, Rudolf (1970), *Theology of the New Testament: Complete in One Volume*, London: Prentice Hall

Camus, Albert (1960), *The Collected Fiction*, London: Hamish Hamilton

— (1942), *Le Mythe de Sisyphe* (trans *The Myth of Sisyphus*), London: Hamish Hamilton

Camus, Albert (1951), *L'Homme révolté* (trans *The Rebel*),
London: Hamish Hamilton

Chesterton, G. K. (1908), *Orthodoxy*, London: Bodley Head

— (1925), *The Everlasting Man*, London: Hodder &
Stoughton

— (1926), *The Catholic Church and Conversion*, San
Francisco: Ignatius Press

— (1929), *The Thing*, London: Sheed & Ward

— (1935), *The Well and the Shallows*, London: Sheed & Ward

Cupitt, Don (1984), *The Sea of Faith*, London: SCM Press

Dawkins, Richard (2006), *The God Delusion*, London:
Bantam Books

Dewart, Leslie (1963), *The Future of Belief*, New York: Herder
& Herder

Duffy, Eamon (2011), *Ten Popes Who Shook the World*,
London: BBC & Yale University Press

Dunne, John S. (1977), *A Search for God in Time and
Memory*, University of Notre Dame Press

Freud, Sigmund (1927), *The Future of an Illusion*, London:
Penguin Books

— (1939), *Moses and Monotheism*, Eastford, Connecticut:
Martino Fine Books

Geering, Lloyd (1980), *Faith's New Age*, London: Collins

Gilbey, A. N. (1983), *We Believe*, London: Bellew Publishing
Company Limited

Howell, Michael; Ford, Peter (1983), *The Illustrated True
History of the Elephant Man*, London: Allison & Busby

Hume, David (1779), *Dialogues Concerning Natural Religion
and the Natural History of Religion*, Oxford World's
Classics

Jenkins, David E. (1966), *The Glory of Man*, London: SCM

Knox, Ronald (1918), *A Spiritual Aeneid*, London: Longmans

— (1927), *The Belief of Catholics*, San Francisco: Ignatius Press

Le Fort, Gertrud von (1931), *Die Letzte am Schafott* (trans *The Song at the Scaffold*), London: Sheed & Ward

Lewis, C. S. (1940), *The Problem of Pain*, London: HarperCollins

— (1942), *The Screwtape Letters*, London: HarperCollins

— (1952), *Mere Christianity*, London: HarperCollins

— (1960), *The Four Loves*, London: Collins

Macquarrie, John (1970*), God-Talk: An Examination of the Language and Logic of Theology*, London: SCM Press

Mayor, F. M. (1913), *The Third Miss Symons*, London: Virago Press

— (1924), *The Rector's Daughter*, London: Virago Press

McCoy, Alban (2004), *An Intelligent Person's Guide to Christian Ethics*, London: Continuum

— (2005), *An Intelligent Person's Guide to Catholicism*, London: Continuum

Newman, Blessed John Henry (1864), *Apologia pro Vita Sua*, New York: Dover Publications

— (1845), *Essay on the Development of Doctrine*, London: Longmans

— (1870), *Essay in Aid of a Grammar of Assent*, London: Longmans

O'Connor, Flannery (1952), *Wise Blood*, New York: Farrar, Straus & Giroux

— (1960), *The Violent Bear It Away*, New York: Farrar, Straus & Giroux

O'Connor, Flannery (1962), *Mystery and Manners*, New York: Farrar, Straus & Giroux

— (1979), *The Habit of Being: Letters* selected and edited by Sally Fitzgerald, New York: Farrar, Straus & Giroux

— (1971), *The Complete Short Stories*, New York: Farrar, Straus & Giroux

Pannenberg, Wolfhart (1977), *Faith and Reality*, London: Westminster Press

Pascal, Blaise (1670), *Pensées*, London: Penguin Books

Plantinga, Alvin (2011), *Where the Conflict Really Lies: Science, Religion, & Naturalism*, Oxford University Press

Rahner, Karl (1978), *Foundations of Christian Faith*, New York: Crossroad Publishing Co

Ramsey, Ian (1957), *Religious Language: An Empirical Placing of Theological Phrases*, London: SCM Press

Ratzinger, Joseph (see Benedict XVI, Pope)

Robinson, Richard (1964), *An Atheist's Values*, Oxford University Press

Russell, Bertrand (1928), *Sceptical Essays*, London: George Allen & Unwin

— (1957), *Why I Am Not A Christian and Other Essays on Religion and Related Subjects*, edited by Paul Edwards, London: George Allen & Unwin

Sartre, Jean-Paul (1943), *L'Être et le Néant* (trans *Being and Nothingness*), London: Methuen

— (1946), *L'existentialisme est un humanisme* (trans *Existentialism and Humanism*), London: Methuen

Sayers, Dorothy L. (1941), *The Mind of the Maker*, London: Methuen

— (1946), *Unpopular Opinions*, London: Victor Gollancz

Sayers, Dorothy L. (1949), *Creed or Chaos?*, New England: Sophia Institute Press

Schweitzer, Albert (1906), *The Quest for the Historical Jesus*, New York: Dover Publications

Smith, Ronald Gregor (1969), *The Free Man: Studies in Christian Anthropology*, London: Collins

Tillich, Paul (1952), *The Courage To Be*, Yale University Press

Tolkien, J. R. R. (1954), *The Lord of the Rings*, London: George Allen & Unwin

Weatherhead, Leslie D. (1945), *A Plain Man Looks at the Cross*, Nashville, Tennessee: Abingdon

Resources

Catechism of the Catholic Church, London: Geoffrey Chapman

Compendium of the Social Doctrine of the Church, London: Continuum

Suggested Further Reading

Barron, Robert (2011), *Catholicism: A Journey to the Heart of the Faith*, New York: Image Books

Benedict XVI, Pope (1971), *Faith and the Future*, San Francisco: Ignatius Press

— (2005), *Christianity and the Crisis of Cultures*, San Francisco: Ignatius Press

Benedict XVI, Pope & Habermas, Jürgen (2005), *The Dialectics of Secularization: On Reason and Religion*, San Francisco: Ignatius Press

Berdyaev, Nicolas (1937), *The Destiny of Man*, London: Geoffrey Bles

Berdyaev, Nicolas (1939), *Spirit and Reality*, London: Geoffrey Bles

Blondel, Maurice (1964), *The Letter on Apologetics* and *History and Dogma*, trans with an introduction by Alexander Dru and Illtyd Trethowan, London: Harvill Press

Boyce Gibson, A. (1970), *Theism and Empiricism*, London: SCM

Calderisi, Robert (2013), *Earthly Mission: The Catholic Church and World Development*, London: Yale University Press

Daniélou, Jean (1961), *Scandaleuse Vérité* (trans *The Scandal of Truth*), London: Burns & Oates

d'Arcy, Martin (1946), *Belief and Reason*, London: Burns & Oates

de Lubac, Henri (1938*) Catholicisme: les aspects sociaux du dogme* (trans *Catholicism: A Study of Dogma in Relation to the Corporate Destiny of Mankind*), London: Burns & Oates

Eliot, T. S. (1939), *The Idea of a Christian Society*, London: Faber & Faber

Geach, Peter (1977), *The Virtues*, Cambridge University Press

Hahn, Scott (2007), *Reasons to Believe*, New York: Doubleday

Hallett, Garth L (2000), *A Middle Way to God*, Oxford University Press

Hart, David Bentley (2009), *Atheist Delusions*, London: Yale University Press

— (2013), *The Experience of God: Being, Consciousness, Bliss*, London: Yale University Press

Hebblethwaite, Brian (2005), *In Defence of Christianity*, Oxford University Press

Hendra, Tony (2004), *Father Joe: The Man Who Saved My Soul*, London: Hamish Hamilton

John Paul II, Pope, *Fides et Ratio* (trans *Faith and Reason*) – encyclical

Knox, Ronald (1932), *Broadcast Minds*, London: Sheed & Ward

— (1942), *In Soft Garments*, San Francisco: Ignatius Press

— (1952), *The Hidden Stream: Mysteries of the Christian Faith*, San Francisco: Ignatius Press

Kreeft, Peter (2014), *Letters to an Atheist*, Plymouth: Rowman & Littlefield

Langmead Casserley, J. V. (1955), *Graceful Reason*, London: Longmans

Layman, C. Stephen (2007), *Letters to Doubting Thomas: A Case for the Existence of God*, Oxford University Press

Lewis, C. S. (1946), *The Great Divorce*, London: Geoffrey Bles

— (1943), *The Abolition of Man*, Oxford University Press

— (1961), *A Grief Observed*, London: Faber & Faber

— (1967), *Christian Reflections*, London: Geoffrey Bles

— (1972), *Undeceptions: Essays on Theology and Ethics*, London: Geoffrey Bles

Lunn, Arnold (1936), *Within That City*, London: Sheed & Ward

MacIntyre, Alistair (1966), *A Short History of Ethics*, London: Routledge & Kegan Paul

Markham, Ian (1998), *Truth and the Reality of God*, Edinburgh: T&T Clark

— (2010), *Against Atheism*, Chichester: Wiley-Blackwell

McGrath, Alister (1999), *The Journey*, London: Hodder & Stoughton

McGrath, Alister (2004), *The Twilight of Atheism: The Rise and Fall of Disbelief in the Modern World*, London: Random House

— (2009), *Heresy: A History of Defending the Truth*, New York: HarperCollins

— (2009), *A Fine Tuned Universe: The Quest for God in Science and Theology*, Louisville, Kentucky: The Westminster John Knox Press

Merton, Thomas (1948), *The Seven Storey Mountain*, London: Sheldon Press

Mitchell, Basil (1973), *The Justification of Religious Belief*, London: Macmillan

— (1980), *Morality: Religious and Secular*, Oxford University Press

Nichols, Aidan (1991), *A Grammar of Consent: The Existence of God in Christian Tradition*, University of Notre Dame Press

O'Leary, Don (2006), *Roman Catholicism and Modern Science*, New York: Continuum

Owens, Joseph (1990), *Towards A Christian Philosophy*, Washington DC: The Catholic University of America Press

Pearce, Joseph (2013), *Race With the Devil: My Journey from Racial Hatred to Rational Love*, Charlotte, North Carolina: St Benedict Press

Plantinga, Alvin (2000), *Warranted Christian Belief*, Oxford University Press

Polkinghorne, John (1996), *Beyond Science*, Cambridge University Press

Poole, Michael (2009), *The 'New' Atheism: 10 Arguments That Don't Hold Water*, Oxford: Lion Hudson

Sayers, Dorothy L. (1943), *The Man Born To Be King*, London: Victor Gollancz

Schönborn, Christoph (2007), *Chance or Purpose? Creation, Evolution, and a Rational Faith*, San Francisco: Ignatius Press

Schumacher, E. F. (1977), *A Guide for the Perplexed*, London: Jonathan Cape

Sheed, F. J. (1947), *Theology and Sanity*, London: Sheed & Ward

Spencer, Nick (2014), *Atheists: The Origin of the Species*, London: Bloomsbury

Swinburne, Richard (1977), *The Coherence of Theism*, Oxford University Press

— (1992), *Revelation*, Oxford University Press

— (2008), *Was Jesus God?*, Oxford University Press

Teilhard de Chardin, Pierre (1966) *Je m'explique* (trans *Let Me Explain*), London: Collins

Trethowan, Dom Illtyd (1970), *Absolute Value: A Study in Christian Theism*, London: George Allen & Unwin

Turner, Denys (2004), *Faith, Reason and the Existence of God*, Cambridge University Press

van Inwagen, Peter (2006), *The Problem of Evil*, Oxford University Press

Weigel, George (2001), *The Truth of Catholicism*, New York: HarperCollins

— (2002), *The Courage To Be Catholic*, New York: Basic Books

— (2013), *Evangelical Catholicism*, New York: Basic Books

Wiebe, Phillip H. (2004), *God and Other Spirits*, Oxford University Press

Williams, Rowan (2007), *Tokens of Trust: An Introduction to Christian Belief*, Canterbury Press

— (2012), *Faith in the Public Square*, London: Bloomsbury

— (2014), *The Edge of Words: God and the Habits of Language*, London: Bloomsbury